education

D1071496

Ed.

french in the elementary school

french in the elementary school

five years' experience

harold b. dunkel and roger a. pillet

the university of chicago press

chicago and london

Library of Congress Catalog Card Number: 62-12631

THE UNIVERSITY OF CHICAGO PRESS, CHICAGO & LONDON
The University of Toronto Press, Toronto 5, Canada

contents

1   planning the program

In the fall of 1955, instruction in foreign languages was restored as part of the regular curriculum of the University of Chicago Elementary School. All third and fourth grade students then in the school began the study of French. In the intervening years, these students have completed the elementary-school program in French.

The following pages are largely an account of our experience. We shall set forth what we tried to do, our reasons for so doing, and the means whereby we sought to do it. We shall indicate the problems and difficulties we encountered and the best solutions we were able to achieve for them. We shall offer the best evidence, objective and otherwise, we have been able to collect on the results of the program. But we made our plans and executed them in the context of thought and action by others working in this field. Consequently, we shall discuss generally most of the major viewpoints and current issues in the field and then give our experience or opinions against this background. The notes at the end of each chapter are devoted primarily to references which sketch this background in greater detail.

The local situation. — Foreign languages had once been a part of the curriculum of the University of Chicago Elementary School for many years, but these courses had been discontinued for a variety of reasons. The decision to reinstitute the language programs and the steps taken to implement it were likewise the product of a number of factors, some of which had considerable influence on the nature of the program actually developed.

Interest in having foreign languages taught in the school had never waned on the part of some members of the university and school faculties, nor on the part of the parent group. Thus the program was seen by many people involved, not as an introduction, but as the long desired resumption of an earlier tradition. Second, under the influence of the Modern Language Association, considerable interest had been generated throughout the country in the Foreign Languages in the Elementary School (or FLES) program. This movement interacted with a third factor — the fact that the administrative organization of the University Elementary and High Schools was at that time being revised in an effort to bring them into closer relation with the research and training interests of the university faculty. To certain members of the faculty the current interest in FLES seemed to suggest a worthwhile research effort. Though many schools and school systems were introducing foreign languages into the early grades, many of these undertakings seemed to be conceived in haste and executed by improvisation. Furthermore, relatively few of these programs were likely to be subjected to much detailed and objective evaluation. Thus the reintroduction of foreign languages into the curriculum of the University Elementary School appeared as an opportunity, not merely to offer language training to our pupils, but also to afford an opportunity for interesting and useful research. Hence, from the very outset, the program was "experimental," not in the sense merely of trying something new, but in the sense that operations were to be scrutinized and measured within the limits of feasibility.

The University Elementary School is certainly not a typical school, and our FLES program has probably not been a typical FLES program for many of the same reasons. FLES programs, as we have learned of them, have been of many different kinds. We believe that this variation is desirable. The kind of language program offered in a school should, like other parts of the curriculum, be appropriate to the setting (both inside and outside the school) within which it is afforded. We do not, consequently, wish to be understood as implying that we believe our FLES program is the only kind of FLES program or the best kind of FLES program that can be offered or that our results are the only kind which can be obtained. Our program was constructed, specifically to fit our situation — as we believe all FLES programs should be. As a result, some aspects of our program are peculiar to our situation; but most of the problems and principles will be common to all FLES programs, and our experience will probably be illuminating to those undertaking similar ventures, even in rather different situations.

Ours is the laboratory school of a university. It is a seven-year elementary school. Though the work of the usual eighth year is presumably distributed throughout the entire curriculum, probably the majority of the extra burden falls in the sixth and seventh (or Prefreshman, as the latter is called) grades.

At the time the experiment began, there were approximately 75 pupils in each grade of the school.

Roughly 50 per cent of the pupils are the children of University of Chicago faculty and staff. A considerable portion of the remainder are the children of professional and business people who have chosen to live in the university neighborhood.

The school has a selective admissions policy. For example, the median IQ is always in the 130's, and very few IQ's in the school fall below 110. IQ is certainly not the most important characteristic of children and certainly not the most vital one in regard to language study. It has often been pointed out that the hotel porter, the waiter, and the lady of easy virtue are often practical linguists of fair competence within limits, though they are not intellectual giants. Moreover, our own evidence (to be reported in a later chapter) corroborates the long list of research findings indicating that IQ is not one of the main prerequisites for speaking and understanding a foreign language. Nonetheless, IQ has some bearing on what is more feasible and justifiable in language instruction and is more succinctly reported than some other factors which enter into the selection of pupils. But other matters, such as the fact that the students come from families willing and able to pay fairly high tuition charges for these particular students, must also not be left out of account.

The bulk of the elementary school students will enter the University High School, and the vast majority of its graduates (better than 90 per cent) will eventually go on to college, with large numbers continuing into graduate schools.

This picture of continuity within the university schools has been somewhat altered by a transiency which has marked all university communities in recent years. The many fellowship and exchange programs have taken many university professors and their families from the community for varying periods, and similarly many visitors have entered the community and the school temporarily for similar reasons. Quite probably the degree of transiency has not been larger than that of many suburban communities where the upwardly mobile junior executive has moved in and out with his family. But two points should be made in connection with this turnover. First, this mobility has produced considerable attrition in the size of our groups over the five years of the experiment. Second, in a program like ours which has stressed the cumulative development of the language skills, this shifting student population has produced special problems in placement and scheduling. Against this second point may be offset the fact that the very number of transfer students into the school made them a large enough problem to make special treatment numerically feasible; a school with fewer such students might find them a nagging problem but one too small to make possible special treatment. Nonetheless, transiency, with its consequences for scheduling and grouping have "muddied" our data even more than we had originally feared.

In short, the pupils in our experiment tend to be children of better than average scholastic ability and interest, drawn from families in the middle class and above, most of whom have intellectual interests and accomplishments of their own and who have intellectual and social aspirations for their children.

The preceding are some of the more important elements in the local situation which influenced the program. Additional ones which are more specifically relevant to particular aspects of the program will be discussed in conjunction with those topics.

The preceding statements may make the pupils in our school appear as very paragons. But there is the other side to the coin. Some of the children are in a private school primarily because they did not fit into their local public school situation. To be sure, sometimes the difficulty was merely that the work of the particular room was not sufficiently challenging. But there are other problems. For example, the fact that our pupils are predominantly drawn from professional, middle-class or better, homes has its obvious advantages. But wealthy and distinguished parents are not necessarily the best parents, and distinguished parents do not always have equally distinguished children. These facts produce strains which have academic consequences for our pupils and for our program.

Moreover, some of the very virtues of a great many of our pupils can actually be a source of difficulty in a subject like language learning. These highly intelligent, highly verbal, creative students often find the step-by-step process involved in language mastery either unfamiliar or uncongenial. Much of their customary academic success has come from relying on intelligence and insight rather than on diligence and concentration — on figuring problems out, on devising new procedures, on presenting their views clearly and persuasively. None of these procedures is particularly helpful in elementary language learning. They won't produce the needed pattern or the needed word in the foreign language. The result is sometimes not merely lower achievement than might be expected, but also a feeling of frustration, with its usual by-products. Thus our results will reflect the achievement of something considerably less than an optimal group of learners for this kind of study. In our own classes, less well-endowed children who settle down and work at mastering the language consistently outperform much more gifted individuals who keep hoping that their undeniable brilliance will somehow see them through.

Preplanning. — Language programs, perhaps even more than others, are liable to sabotage or indifference. In undertaking this program, rather strenuous efforts were made to gain the advice and consent of the fairly large number of varied groups involved in some fashion. A University of Chicago seminar in educational psychology engaged in studying decision-making undertook as a class project investigating the decision to reintroduce foreign languages into the Elementary School. When these students inquired of the various groups involved who was primarily responsible for the decision, their findings indicated that each group felt that *it* was.* And certainly the mere execution of the program, to say nothing of such success as it has had, would have been impossible without the active co-operation of members of all these groups.

The first step was to gain the assent of the Board of Precollegiate Education, the university ruling body which serves in somewhat the function of a school board for the university's schools below the collegiate level. With their consent, and even urging, Dunkel, as Director of Precollegiate Education, then appointed an advisory committee for the project. This committee contained representatives of the following groups: all the language departments of the high school, the college and the graduate school, including the Oriental Institute and the departments of linguistics and anthropology; the administration of the school, and the Board of Precollegiate Education. In addition to their obvious professional expertness, this advisory committee contributed considerable knowledge about various programs past and present and about possible personnel for the program. This committee through frequent meetings carried the burden of the original discussion and planning. Then as tentative decisions were reached, these were referred to the Policy Committee and the total faculty of the school for further reworking. As precise plans took definite shape, the parent group was kept informed through its newsletter and through meetings. As a result, by the time the program had actually begun, everyone knew just about as much as there was to know, and the general plan had benefited by suggestions from a wide variety of sources.

In this connection it is important to point out that the continuance of the program has depended on the whole-

* We are indebted to our colleague, J. W. Getzels, for this information on his seminar.

hearted support of Herbert Schooling and Roy Larmee, who followed Dunkel as Directors of Precollegiate Education, and of Robert Ohm, the principal of the school. FLES programs by their very nature become increasingly expensive and complicated as they grow to their full size, and the reluctant administrator can always find plausible excuses for discontinuing them. Without complete administrative co-operation, no FLES program can flourish.

We owe a similar debt of gratitude to the entire faculty of the school. Their co-operation has been, quite literally, unbelievable. They have all gladly helped when called upon for assistance of various kinds. Probably even more difficult, they have cheerfully borne the host of minor inconveniences and dislocations which the French program has imposed on their professional daily lives over the years.

Objectives. — It seemed extremely important that our program should stress competence in the linguistic skills: i.e., the ability to speak, understand, read and write a foreign language. For students to attain these skills in varying degrees was the chief goal of our program.

FLES courses in general cover a wide range of various combinations of objectives. Other programs, though they do not ignore the basic linguistic aims may quite properly give them minor emphasis because these courses stress other objectives such as the daily life and culture of the foreign country (particularly the life of children there with their songs, games, and dances). In fact, some programs are essentially social studies courses, with very little emphasis on the mastery of the foreign language. With such programs we certainly have no quarrel. For many schools in many situations courses of these other sorts are probably the most appropriate type. Certainly they avoid many difficulties which our sort of program entails. They can be easily handled in the self-contained classroom even if the teacher's knowledge of the foreign language is extremely limited. Also, all students can advance as a group, without the cumulative nature of language achievement causing trouble as students progress at varying rates.

For our situation, however, primary emphasis on the linguistic skills seemed the only possible choice. We had clear indications from many sources that if our students had studied something that was called "foreign language" for four or five years in elementary school, students, parents, and faculty would assume that considerable linguistic competence had been acquired. Furthermore, this achievement would have to be documented by the advanced standing awarded when the student ultimately reached the high school. Failure in this regard had apparently been one of the reasons for the discontinuance of the former classes, and any program which failed to produce this kind of facility would sooner or later run into severe local opposition.

We faced this ultimate evaluation in the full realization that talk concerning language instruction is usually couched in terms of "years" and that "year" is an ambiguous and unfair term as applied to elementary-school programs. When one speaks of "years of foreign language study," the speaker generally has in mind the block of time available in high-school or college instruction. But there the class "hour" is usually fifty minutes. In our program the "hour" was going to be only fifteen minutes or so at the lower grades. Thus, measured in terms of actual clock-hours, our five years would constitute a very small total. In addition, the amount of further contact with the language provided by outside preparation for class would be similarly limited at these levels. Despite these inequalities inherent in the calculation, however, we saw that students, parents, and colleagues would expect that students, after four or five such years of study, should have a fairly good command of the language.

As a general principle of language study and as one particularly appropriate to work in the elementary grades, we believed that the student should begin with speaking and hearing the language. Among the primary reasons for beginning foreign language instruction in the elementary grades is the fact that younger learners acquire the spoken language more easily than older ones. Their muscular and mental habits are less fixed; and children are less self-conscious about imitating strange sounds and making funny mistakes than are adolescents. Moreover, since the children in the lower grades are just mastering the reading and writing of their native language, an oral-aural approach to the foreign one prevents their having to cope with two orthographies simultaneously.

This stress on speaking and understanding is justified, however, on more grounds than the fact that these skills are particularly feasible for younger children or the theoretical principle that speech is prior to writing. The various factors in the modern world which have made foreign travel and foreign residence commonplace have given a new significance to the oral-aural skills. Many more people than ever before will have the opportunity and the need to converse in the language they study. Then too, the early start gives some assurance that the student can work with the language long enough to gain an oral mastery of it. (After all it was the brevity of the average student's course which led some decades ago to the concentration on the easiest of the objectives, the ability to read.) In sum, because the audio-lingual skills had a new importance and because a FLES program has an unusual opportunity to enable the student to master them, we wished to begin with speaking and understanding the language and to continue this emphasis as long as possible.

But however long that period could be, the problems of reading and writing had to be faced. This is a "problem" for several reasons, the most important of which for present purposes is the fact that French orthography is not a simple transcription of the sounds of the language. Thus an oral knowledge of the word does not tell the students how to spell it; and conversely, a "spelling pronunciation" engendered by the sight of a normal text can undermine previously acquired habits of accurate pronunciation.

Despite these complications we saw that the transition to reading and writing would need to be made fairly early for several reasons. First, students of this age, who have just mastered the reading and writing of their native language, are likely to attach considerable importance to written materials and are inclined to demand them in a second language. Second, work at the high-school level usually emphasizes written materials; FLES students who could not handle them would be at a disadvantage (despite any greater oral-aural competence they might have), and on this basis the elementary program might be deemed a waste of time. Third, written materials could be used to extend the student's contact with the language outside class. We were not equipped with tapes, records, or the like which the student could take home, and we had no language laboratory for after-school use. Since these facilities were being provided in a new building planned and built during the five years covered here, a temporary installation was out of the question. Hence, apart from some phonetic transcriptions which could be made available on a limited basis (with their inherent difficulty that, in the eyes of older students and parents, "That really isn't French"), the student's exposure to the language would be limited almost exclusively to classroom time until the transition to written materials could be made. Finally, there was also the possibility that not all students would be able to learn the language by oral-aural means. The fact that everyone learns his native language in this fashion is only partially, and even faintly, relevant to the situation in which an older learner studies language for a few minutes a day as one of several school subjects. In our kind of civilization and educational system, some students apparently become "eye-minded" very early. As we shall indicate later, we found that some few of the students who did poorly while instruction was completely oral-aural, improved once written materials were introduced.

Thus reading and writing came second in our program only in time and not in emphasis for the total period. We sought to give our students the advantages of being able to read the technical, belletristic and journalistic materials available in the foreign language.

Cultural matters, though not emphasized, were certainly not neglected. The country, its people and their life, its history, and its arts all figured in the materials used. But these points were ancillary to the teaching of the language or supplementary to it rather than the other way around as in some FLES programs.

It is worth pointing out that our students are present and future members of the intellectual and social groups most likely to find mastery of the language valuable. They are the group most likely to live and travel abroad. Their future careers and patterns of life are likely to be those which make the ability to read a foreign language and the knowledge of a foreign culture meaningful and even necessary. On this basis, we see our kind of program as fitting our school and our students, but we doubt its appropriateness to all other situations. For the same reasons, we have stoutly resisted dogmas which would suggest that other types of FLES programs effective elsewhere must serve as models for ours.

General plan. — The original plan was that foreign language instruction should begin in the fourth grade and should be offered to all students. It did not seem to the advisory committee that foreign languages should be an optional study. We believed that if foreign languages were a suitable study for the elementary school, they should be available to all children, just as in our school all children take science, mathematics and the rest. We were also uneasy about use of foreign languages as a subject for "enrichment." Unusual intellectual ability did not seem to be required, and consequently it did not seem appropriate to have language study be an extra plum in the elementary curriculum.

Since ours is a seven-year elementary school, beginning at the fourth grade would have given the student four years of study before entering high school. In discussions with the school's faculty, however, many of the teachers at the lower grades suggested that the third grade was equally appropriate and perhaps even more suitable as a starting point.

Some consideration was also given to the possibility of a still earlier start. Certainly the child learns his native language at a much earlier age. But he learns his native language in a family and in a community where this language is spoken continually by everyone. Under similar circumstances, the achievements of young children who acquire a foreign language while living among native speakers of it are familiar. The situation is markedly different, however, when the foreign language is merely a "subject" in nursery school, kindergarten, or the primary grades.

Since some of the alleged advantages of an earlier start did not seem to apply, we felt free to worry about some possible disadvantages. First, there seemed to us the danger that the youthful student would get the much too easily acquired feeling "I've already had that for a couple of years" and that too early introduction might simply take the edge off interest and enthusiasm without producing compensatory results. Second, at the primary grades, the student is learning to read and write his native tongue. There seemed some possibility — and not a remote one — that the introduction of another linguistic system might cause some confusion, particularly for pupils already having difficulty with the symbolization of their mother tongue.

The upshot of these deliberations was that instruction in French was begun by all students at both the third and fourth grades in 1955. In 1956, all entering students automatically took German as that program was inaugurated. In subsequent years, the students in the third grade were offered a choice of either French or German, and students transferring into the school at later grades were placed in appropriate sections of whichever language they elected, as will be indicated in a later chapter.

Choice of language. — The question of which language to teach was naturally one which early confronted the advisory committee and the school faculty. Both groups were prepared to make the professional decision that foreign languages should enter the curriculum of the elementary school. When it became a question of "Which language?" both groups were far from doctrinaire. We were well aware, for example, of the advantages of a non-Indo-European language on a number of theoretical and practical grounds. But the improbability of securing teachers adequately trained in such languages and also competent to work with third- and fourth-grade students as well as the almost surmountable difficulties of obtaining appropriate elementary materials for three or four years' work rapidly removed these more exotic languages from actual consideration, regardless of the admitted validity of their claims. Because of the appropriateness of an aural-oral emphasis for this age-group, the classical languages seemed less fitting than one of the modern ones. The question thus resolved itself into which of the major modern Indo-European languages should be taught. At this point, since the question seemed to the committee and the faculty principally to be a matter of personal preference rather than one of professional judgment, the children's parents were polled. They were asked to indicate a preference between French, German, Spanish, Italian and Russian. In this popularity contest, French won out. Parents, however, indicated that they were in essentially the same position as the faculty, for, almost without exception, they indicated that if the language or languages of their choice were not selected, they would be glad to have their child take any other one on the list.

Time. — Several matters having to do with time became extremely important at this point.

The first of these was the necessity for continuity. Though a year or two of foreign language, the study of which is never continued or is resumed only three or four years later, may produce valuable and measurable results, we felt this outcome was highly unlikely in a course like ours which would stress the language skills. (Possibly courses which give greater stress to the cultural aspects of the foreign country or to changing attitudes toward foreign languages and peoples may leave a greater residue in these circumstances.) We believed it of primary importance, consequently, that both we and the children should undertake the program as a continuous one, that is, that students starting French in the third grade should have the opportunity to continue French uninterruptedly through the elementary-school years. We have carried out that part of the program.

Another aspect of the problem of time was raised by the question, "Where can we find the time in the school day?" If foreign languages were to be added to the curriculum, what was to be forced out? The elementary curriculum is certainly crowded. If, however, one undertakes to point out subjects which one feels are unimportant and/or frivolous, another member of the committee is quick to indicate that he regards these subjects as having great theoretical or practical desirability. In this kind of debate, clearly one man's meat is another man's poison.

When this problem was placed frankly before the school's faculty, the home-room teachers came up with the admirable and very workable suggestion that it should be left to each of them to squeeze in the time as he saw fit. This they did as best fitted the progress of their class and the particular state of their own daily schedules. Possibly in some cases, time was utilized which would have been essentially wasted. In most cases, however, teachers have probably stolen a bit of time from a variety of activities in order to make room for foreign languages. Though each home-room teacher solved this problem in his own way, the total effect was admirably satisfactory. Time was found. As the periods for foreign language instruction became longer for the later grades, other devices were used such as squeezing the lunch hour or extending the school day. In no case, however, has some other subject had to be crowded out of the curriculum in order to make room for foreign languages.

The mode of operation just mentioned has had, of course, its bearing on another aspect of time, in the sense of "length of class hour." During the first year of the program, it seemed appropriate that approximately fifteen minutes should be used. This seemed as much as could be conveniently squeezed into a busy schedule. This also seemed about the length of time that children with the attention span of third-graders could effectively give to instruction in a foreign language. In the best of all possible worlds, a slightly longer period would probably have been desirable. A certain amount of time is always lost in getting things started — in distributing materials and performing other classroom tasks. To take care of these necessary operations and also to provide adequate instruction has required a rather brisk effort on the part of the language teachers. A somewhat longer period would have made possible a somewhat more relaxed approach. Be that as it may, fifteen minutes worked rather well and seemed to be about adequate for the third-grade student. The fourth graders were apparently capable of longer attention to this kind of material and, of course, in subsequent years of the program, the length of time given foreign languages was increased.

Teachers. — In planning the program, it seemed very important to us that the teachers should be native speakers of the language or native speakers of English who had acquired a reasonable facsimile of a native French pronunciation. Hence, insofar as possible, we sought native speakers of the language, who were competent to teach it, and who were able to work with American elementary-school children. Over the years, as our program has grown, we have not always been able to meet all these criteria adequately. This problem is common to all FLES programs; and the fact that in an urban and university situation such as ours we have had difficulty in solving it adequately is some indication of the difficulty which schools less fortunately situated will have in staffing their programs.

Fortunately for our immediate purposes, the University Elementary School was not organized on the basis of the self-contained classroom. Hence a special teacher for foreign languages would be no anomaly in a school already familiar with special teachers for art, science, and a number of other subjects, and we planned our program to function in this way.

Materials. — At the time our program began, materials for FLES were beginning to become available. But they were likely to be deficient in quantity for a program as long as ours, and much of this material would be intended for objectives and situations other than ours. We realized, therefore, that one of the heaviest commitments in undertaking the program was the preparation of an adequate bulk of appropriate and usable materials. The details of this problem will be discussed in a later chapter.

Method. — We were not doctrinaire in our attitude toward methods and were prepared to be what is generally labeled "eclectic." Eclecticism is usually frowned upon because it usually denotes the more or less arbitrary snatching of isolated fragments from various comprehensive theories and dumping the odds and ends thus selected into a mishmash. But most "theories" or "methods" of language teaching are not coherent and comprehensive wholes. Often they are the inflation of a partial truth, good enough as far as it goes, into what is alleged to be a total theory — which it is not. A program which makes any claim to comprehensiveness, therefore, must use several of them as mutual supplements to each other.

Research and evaluation. — As was indicated earlier, one

17

of our chief reasons for undertaking a FLES program was the opportunity it offered for research in this area. Within the obvious limits of a single program of a particular type in a rather atypical situation, we wished to get the best answers we could to some of the problems troubling everyone interested in foreign language teaching at this level. From the outset, therefore, we undertook to collect as much varied information as we could. The details will be given in later chapters.

But we also were operating within a school. We had to provide adequate instruction for all the children involved and to function within the framework of the policies and organization of the school. At numerous points, consequently, what would have been experimentally desirable had to yield to what was practically necessary. In this respect our program is no different from most others. But these pressures have made our design and our data less than adequate at some obvious points.

With this much picture of the situation at the start of the program, we can turn to more extended treatment of various aspects of it.

notes to chapter 1

The references in the following notes are not intended as an extensive bibliography on FLES or a general introduction to the topic. Readers seeking the first are referred to Evelyn Eenenaam's annual "Annotated Bibliography of Modern Language Methodology" in the *Modern Language Journal* or Roger Pillet's section on "Foreign Languages" in the *Elementary School Journal's* "Selected References on Elementary School Instruction." An extremely useful source of information on rationale, methods and materials for FLES is Marjorie Johnston and Ilo Remer, *References on Foreign Languages in the Elementary School* ("U. S. Department of Health, Education and Welfare, Circular No. 495 [Revised]" [Washington: U. S. Office of Education, 1959]). Anyone seeking a general overview of the subject should read such books as Theodore Andersson, *The Teaching of Foreign Language in the Elementary School,* (Preliminary Edition) Boston: D. C. Heath, 1953; and Nelson Brooks, *Language and Language Learning,* (New York: Harcourt Brace, 1960).

Rather, one purpose of these notes is to suggest some of the variety of purpose, opinion, and plan which has marked the various FLES programs and thus to show the position of our program amid others. A second purpose is to indicate more extended discussions of some issues than we felt were appropriate here.

P. 2. *FLES program.* — The growth of FLES can best be understood if seen in the broader context of the resurgent interest in foreign language at all educational levels: William R. Parker, *The National Interest and Foreign Languages* (Discussion Guide and Work Paper for Citizen Consultation Initiated by the U.S. National Commission for UNESCO. Dept. of State, [Washington: U.S. Government Printing Office, 1957]).
The rationale for the extension of foreign-language instruction to the grades is well summarized in Kenneth Mildenberger, "World Affairs, Languages, and Children," *College of Education Quarterly* (Michigan State University), IV (October, 1958), 22–27.

P. 2. *Reintroduction of foreign languages.* — Concern for better evidence on some vital questions arising in connection with FLES has been recently voiced in two articles: John B. Carroll, "Teaching Foreign Languages to Children: What Research Shows," *National Elementary Principal,* XXXIX (May, 1960), 12–15; and "Wanted: A Research Basis for Educational Policy on Foreign Language Teaching," *Harvard Educational Review,* XXX (Spring, 1960), 128–40.

P. 3. *Kind of language program offered.* — See Harold B. Dunkel, "A Few Facts about Foreign-Language Study," *Elementary School Journal,* LIX (October, 1958), 31–34.

P. 8. Certain questions (Why? When? To whom?) about the institution of FLES are inevitable. Some recent expositions of these questions and of the essentials for a successful FLES program are the following: George Denemark, and Wesley J. Matson, "Teach Children a Foreign Language?" *National Elementary Principal,* XXXIX (May, 1960), 6–11; Dean N. Evans, "Planning for a Foreign-Language Program," *Elementary*

School Journal, LX (October, 1959), 32–36; Paul M. Glaude, "The Establishment of FLES Programs," *Modern Language Journal*, XLIV (April, 1960), 158–59; Arthur E. Hamalainen, "Administering the Foreign Language Program," *National Elementary Principal*, XXXIX (May, 1960), 22–25; Gerald Newmark, "Planning for the Improvement of Foreign Language Experiences in Elementary Schools," *California Journal of Elementary Education*, XXVIII (May, 1960), 223–33.

As can be seen from some of the preceding material, the administrator, even though favorably disposed, is not always so sanguine that the difficulties can be overcome as is the enthusiast for foreign languages. Typical of this position is Donald H. Hughes, "Should We Teach Languages to Children?" *College of Education Quarterly* (Michigan State University), IV (October, 1958), 28–33.

The reasons underlying a decision not to institute a program are reported in "When Should our Children Begin French?" *Independent School Bulletin*, (January, 1959), pp. 8–10;

and a rebuttal appears in Nelson Brooks, "Language Learning in the Grades," *Independent School Bulletin*, (January, 1959), 11–13.

P. 10. Emphasis on a prolonged audio-lingual introduction is generally seen as the essential feature of language teaching in "The new key." In addition to the works of Andersson and Brooks cited at the beginning of this section, see also Marjorie C. Johnston, "The Urgency of Accelerating the Teaching of Foreign Languages 'In the New Key'," *Modern Language Journal*, Vol. XLII (April, 1958), 163–68.

P. 11. *The transition to reading and writing.* – Workers elsewhere, for various reasons, have also suggested modification of the exclusive emphasis on audio-lingual work in FLES: Manuel H. Guerra, "Is Conversation Enough?" *Hispania*, XLIII (May, 1960), 249–52; Arthur S. Trace Jr., "The New Look in Foreign Language Instruction: Threat or Promise," *Modern Language Journal*, XLIII (December, 1959), 382–86; Dorothy P. Foster and Clarence M. Williams, "Aural-Oral-Written Versus Aural-Oral in Teaching Spanish to Fourth Graders," *Modern Language Journal*, XLIV (April, 1960), 153–57; Catherine Bill Osborn, "Necessary Tools for FLES" (Notes and Discussion) *French Review*, XXXI (April, 1958) 438–39.

P. 12. *Cultural matters.* — The extreme position here, arising from lack of confidence in the ability of FLES programs to impart the linguistic skills, sees FLES as concerned primarily with giving informal experience with several languages and cultures, e.g.: Anne S. Hoppock, "Foreign Languages in the Elementary School — How Effective?" *Modern Language Journal,* XLI (October, 1957) 269–71.

P. 13. *Suitable starting point.* — The majority of FLES programs seem to start at either the third or the fourth grade. But the range is very wide, some beginning as early as nursery school or kindergarten and others beginning as late as the seventh or eighth grades, chiefly as downward extensions of high-school programs. The following references, in addition to the comments of Anderson (*op. cit.*, pp. 27–31) and Brooks (*op. cit.*, pp. 112–14), point to the sort of consideration involved: Gertrude Hildreth, "Learning a Second Language in the Elementary Grades and High School," *Modern Language Journal,* XLIII (March, 1959), 136–42; Carl G. F. Franzén, "Foreign Language in the Curriculum," *Bulletin of the School of Education Indiana University,* XXXIV (January, 1958), 1–30; Thérèse Ferault, "L'Enseignement du français au stade élémentaire," *French Review,* XXXIII (February, 1960) 379–88; Max S. Kirch, "At What Age Elementary School Language Teaching?" *Modern Language Journal,* XL (November, 1956), 399–400; Carlos Rivera, "The El Paso Spanish Program: Grade One through Seven," *Hispania,* XLI (May, 1958), 263–65.

P. 13. *The German program.* — See W. Gregor Heggen, "German in the Third and Fourth Grade," *German Quarterly,* XXXI (November, 1958), 298–303.

2   staffing and scheduling

For staffing a FLES program, the two major alternatives are either to have the instruction carried on by the regular home-room teacher or to use a special foreign language teacher. Both approaches have inherent merits as well as defects.

From the point of view of competence in the foreign language the specialist is obviously in a more favorable position and the home-room teacher at an obvious disadvantage because of more limited training. Fluency is of great importance, but major consideration must be given to the teacher's accent since the pupils will imitate a poor accent as readily as a good one.

For programs stressing the oral skills these facts are perhaps decisive in favor of the specialist at the present time. In most schools there simply are not enough regular teachers in the elementary grades who have an adequate command of some one foreign language to make possible a continuous program. But as various mechanical aids are developed, they may compensate for the inadequacies of the regular teacher. We shall present some tentative findings in this regard in a few pages.

If these devices can be made to work, they will enable us to utilize those points at which the regular classroom teacher is superior. For example, until a greater number of language specialists become versed in teaching the elementary grades, the home-room teacher is probably better aware of children's needs and interests and of the best way of making the learning experience productive than is the language specialist. The lower the age level, the more important this knowledge of the proper class room management and correct elementary methods becomes.

A second important advantage (and again, the lower the grade, the more important it is) is the fact that the home-room teacher can avoid any rigid compartmentalization of foreign language instruction. He can operate either with or without a definitely scheduled daily period for instruction; and, regardless of how this initial presentation is made, he can bring in the foreign language at other appropriate times during the day, thus extending the amount of contact with the language, giving it a note of reality by relating it to other subjects, and providing more natural motivation.

A third consideration related to organization rather than to teaching effectiveness is the simplicity of having the home-room teacher schedule his own foreign language class as compared with the two complications at least which arise when a specialist is used. One is that scheduling the foreign language program becomes increasingly difficult as the program expands, especially if other "special" teachers are used for other subjects also. Since the specialist must of necessity spread his activity over most of the school day, he is bound to have some conflicts with classes scheduled for other special teachers. This situation becomes still more troublesome if more than one language is taught in the language program or if any grouping of students is attempted. It becomes extremely difficult to work with groups made up of children from different home rooms, whether at the same or different grade levels, without disturbing the academic activities of the remainder of their respective groups.

A second complication which attends the work of the specialist and which the use of the regular home-room teacher avoids arises from the physical demands made on the teacher by the audio-lingual method (the proper method at the early grade levels). Because of the relative shortness of the class periods, the specialist will probably be expected to carry eight to ten classes a day for a full teaching load. Our own experience has been that, in addition to physical fatigue, tedium inescapably sets in at some point and further reduces the teacher's efficiency. The home-room teacher is not exposed to a similar monotony.

Administratively, the use of the regular teacher has the distinct advantage of obviating the trouble and expense of hiring a staff of specialists.

All these are very real factors which favor the home-room teacher and account for the extended use made of him in programs where his lack of linguistic competence does not make it impossible.

It appears from the literature and from our own observations that the success of this approach depends in great part on the direction given it by some qualified language specialist who should administer the program as to personnel, materials and the general sequence of instruction and insist on sufficient contact hours and continuity of instruction.

If the FLES program is to be staffed by specialists, several sorts of personnel either on a full-time or part-time basis, are possible.

1. A native speaker with proper academic background and experience for teaching at the elementary grades. This type is, of course, the most desirable but, unfortunately, it it is still relatively rare. Until more language teachers are trained specifically for FLES, most teachers who are linguistically competent will be short on elementary-school training and experience. Conversely, when a group of native speakers can be found in the regular teaching corps, they are usually competent in different languages. This fact accounts in part for the many FLES programs in which a year or so of one language has been followed by a year of a different language. For programs (like ours) which aim at increasing mastery of one language, this situation is impossible.

2. A native speaker without formal training or experience. Preferably this should be a person who likes children and is familiar with them from having worked in some organized activity like the Boy Scouts, Sunday school, or day camp. Especially in larger communities, such persons are not uncommon. A problem occurs, of course, because of state or local requirements forbidding the hiring of people lacking appropriate certification. In some cases, these legal regulations have been circumvented by offering the foreign language as a voluntary, extracurricular activity after school. Frequently certifying authorities have been lenient in issuing temporary or emergency licenses, particularly until such potential teachers had time to meet the formal requirements.

3. Foreign language instructors working at higher educational levels and borrowed full time or part time for the elementary school program. Though such teachers are com-

petent in the foreign language, success in teaching at higher levels does not necessarily mean success in teaching at the lower grades. Initial enthusiasm for the elementary project can easily turn to discouragement because of temperament, lack of flexibility, or the assumption that teaching foreign language involves the same attitudes and techniques at all educational levels. If regular high-school or college teachers are used, they should be encouraged to become conversant with the FLES literature and become aware of the special problems before deciding to participate in an elementary-school program.

4. Graduate students in foreign language departments of nearby colleges or universities. Such students are, in theory, very good prospects since they have fair proficiency in the foreign language and are conversant with at least the general problems of classroom management. Their effectiveness is, of course, proportionate to their preparation. That the experience can benefit both the program and the trainee has been reported.

We should, however, like to caution the administrator against two types. One is the apparently zealous graduate student who turns out to be primarily interested in "working his way through college." The second is the student whose interest is real but who, because of the pressures of his own academic work, gradually devotes less and less thought, energy, and time to his instructional obligations.

In any case, in view of the obvious shortage of expert foreign language teachers at the elementary level, the initiate should be given ample opportunity to "find his way" and gradually to increase his effectiveness in the field. For many, the first year will be one of training as well as teaching, and one must be prepared to put up with the faults and difficulties arising from inexperience. Premature concern by administrators or undue pressure by parents because the new teacher is having obvious problems can result in a long-term loss to the program. The novice, feeling undue pressure in one system (which has, in a sense, financially supported his training) can easily turn up the following year as FLES "expert" in a neighboring system, leaving the original system to train another beginner.

Our own staffing has taken the following shape. During the first two years, all classes were taught by Pillet, who is a native speaker of French. While he had had considerable experience in teaching at other levels, he had never before taught in the grades. But before the start of the program he made rather extensive preparation, both in regard to FLES and in regard to general elementary methods.

With program expansion in the third year, another native speaker was added, who has worked with us throughout the remainder of the program. She too had not previously taught at the elementary level, but she had had considerable experience gained through her own three children, two of whom were of the same general age as our pupils. Carrying other work in the school, her load in French FLES was only part time until the fifth year.

In the fourth year, two new staff members were added, also on a part-time basis. One of them was a native speaker who was teaching at the high-school level. He withdrew after one year simply because he did not enjoy teaching younger children. The second addition was a graduate student from the university's French department. He had had no previous teaching experience at all, but had done extensive work with scout and Sunday-school groups. He too left at the end of the fourth year, going to conduct a FLES program elsewhere. In the last year we had another American graduate student without previous teaching experience, who has now completed his graduate work and gone to take a college position.

This pattern of staffing has two obvious characteristics. One is that the bulk of our teaching has been done by native speakers of French who had not had previous experience at the elementary level. Ideally, we should have liked for our staff to have had greater formal training and experience for the lower grades. But since we had to settle for less than perfection, we believed that a fluent command of correct French was the indispensable characteristic for a staff member in a program which emphasizes the audiolingual skills and which then had almost no access to mechanical aids and supplements.

A second feature of our staffing policy has been the use of part-time instructors. The primary reason for this policy will be indicated in chapter 4. It has allowed us to "saturate" certain blocks of time in the daily schedule — the best solution we have found to the difficult problem of scheduling in an elementary program. Part-time teachers concentrating their work at certain vital periods in the school's schedule gave us a coverage at these hours which would not otherwise have been possible. This solution was, of course, made possible primarily because of the proximity of a graduate school which gave us a pool of competent and interested teachers who were glad to work part time. FLES programs in other locations might find it more difficult to staff on this basis and hence more difficult to meet the scheduling problem in this fashion (which we have found very workable).

One of the most frequent questions asked in connection with FLES is "where does the time come from?" Obviously so little as even a daily 15-20 minutes, which is minimal, must replace some other activity in the crowded curriculum. (There are, of course, no complications if foreign languages instruction is given on an elective basis before or after school.)

In our own experience, as indicated earlier, time in the regular school day was made for foreign language instruction in the lower grades by nibbling a little here and there so as not to eliminate or seriously cut into any one area. A careful scrutiny of any daily schedule would probably suggest that 5 minutes less for the lunch period might not be disastrous, that 25 instead of 30 minutes for some subject or activity might not seriously curtail progress in that area, or that transit time from one class to another might be absorbed within the scheduled class time rather than be reflected as a 5-minute break in the schedule.

In the third year of the program instruction was extended from 75 minutes per week to 100 minutes per week. This expansion was possible because 15 minutes were added to the school day. Considerations in the scheduling of other subjects were also involved in making this decision. But the belief that foreign languages should be given adequate attention as part of the regular instructional program played a part. This time was distributed as a 25-minute period four days a week, however, instead of the daily fifteen minutes.

A number of arguments can be used to justify various special efforts to make room for foreign languages, depending, of course, on the type of program involved. If the work in foreign languages is offered as part of an enrichment program providing opportunity for the "gifted," for such children a few minutes less instruction in one or several areas cannot be detrimental since they already excel in these areas with a minimum of time and effort. If the course stresses the life and culture of the countries speaking the languages, the time used for it is properly counted as part of the allowance for the social studies, reading, music or other appropriate parts of the usual curriculum. If the course stresses mastery of the language skills, a strong argument for additional time can be adduced on the ground that early initiation is desirable to the point of necessity for a high level of proficiency in the oral use of the language. Since this is one area in which the young child child has a special competence which may be lost later, the failure to take advantage of it approximates irresponsibility.

As to the frequency of the foreign-language class, we are strongly in favor of daily contact, especially in the lower grades. At this frequency, 15-20 minutes have proved practical for us at the third and fourth grade levels from the point of view of attention span. Twenty-five minutes at the fifth and sixth grade levels certainly does not seem too taxing for the children. At the seventh grade, our lesson pattern changed to two classes per week each of 50 minutes. Although children of this age can handle the longer class, the three to four day gap between language classes has seemed to us far from ideal in promoting sustained effort and consistent progress on the part of the students. But for us, as for everyone else, the scheduling of foreign-language classes has necessarily depended on other curricular considerations at each grade level.

A danger of the shorter period (15 minutes) when the class is conducted by a special language teacher is that it tends to become depersonalized. Under pressure of wishing to get as much done as possible in the brief span, a teacher may be reluctant to give the time necessary for the personal comments and that relaxed atmosphere which are most effective with younger children. Our experience has led us to believe that it is well worthwhile all along the line to sacrifice five minutes of "instruction" to establishing a friendly atmosphere and greater personal contact with the children.

The visiting specialist must also be careful, in spite of his conviction of the value of his subject or his feeling that he has not been given enough time, to adhere scrupulously to his schedule. To arrive late means wasted time for the children and for the home-room teacher (who, ideally, should have got the children "ready" for the language instructor.) To stay late results in throwing the rest of the daily schedule out of line and being criticized for taking more time than had been allowed, perhaps reluctantly, for the foreign language. Co-operation with and from the home-room teacher is an important factor in the success of the foreign language class.

The hour of the day at which the foreign language class can be scheduled depends, of course, on the framework of the total curriculum. In our opinion, the younger the group, the greater need to schedule the foreign-language class in the morning hours when the children are fresh. At the other extreme, our experience has been that for the third and fourth grades, the last hour in the afternoon is an almost completely unproductive time. (To some extent, this fact is true at all levels, but these hours become much more difficult to avoid as the schedule in the upper grades grows still more rigid.) But many subjects have rightful claims to those "better" hours when pupils are not still waking up, digesting their lunches, or tired and ready to go home. Whether the program is taught by the regular teacher or by a specialist, an attitude of reasonable compromise on these matters will, in the long run, contribute to a smoother operation of the program.

In addition to competition from other areas, scheduling can be complicated by factors generated within the foreign language program itself. In our own case, as the school's language program grew we found ourselves dealing with two languages, both taught at each grade level. Later, grouping the students in sections according to achievement further complicated our scheduling problem. Providing for students transferring into the school at various grade levels in unpredictable numbers is another major complication.

May we mention parenthetically that the person in charge of the FLES program can best resolve such problems. Especially in the early stages of a program, administrators or other persons charged with arranging the schedule, while paying lip service to the merits of the program, may be happy to declare it unpractical or more work than it is worth. Someone who knows the requirements of the program and who is sufficiently devoted to it to be willing to spend the time puzzling out the admittedly difficult problems involved must cope with these problems of scheduling.

We have had some success in scheduling language classes by thinking of the population in terms of one or even two whole grade levels, setting aside a block of time for that grade level and completing all the foreign language instruction within that block of time, regardless of language taught or level of instruction. We realize that we have been in the fortunate position of being able to get sufficient part-time staff to enable us to saturate that block of time with classes for a particular level. Furthermore, at our most complicated level (fifth and sixth grades) we have found it expedient (though not ideal) to concentrate the work in a one-hour block of time at noon. All the children at this level have language in one of the half-hours and lunch in the other. This scheduling plan, which has the merit of being flexible while not infringing on other academic activities, is offered merely as one example of what can be done to provide adequate instruction and yet avoid the criticism FLES programs may well encounter if they infringe on too many classes and activities.

| 11:00 | German 4
6th grade

Teacher A | German 4
6th grade

Teacher B | French 1
5th–6th grade
Transfer Students
Teacher C | |
| 11:30 | German 3
(on basis of
ability or
grouping)
Teacher A | French 3
5th–6th
grade (ac-
celerated)
Teacher D | French 3
5th grade

Teacher E | French 2
5th–6th
Last year &
"decelerated"
Teacher C |

The preceding schedule represents a partial solution to the problem of students transferring into the program above the third grade. We have been fortunate in usually having ten to fifteen transfer students at each grade level. By cutting across grade lines, we have made up beginning classes of the combined grade level entrants. On some occasions when the number of transfer students was too small to warrant a section, we have put them in a second-year language class and provided time after school to help them catch up with the group.

Another troublesome problem which complicates scheduling (though it is not mentioned as often as that of the transfer entrants) is that caused by dropouts. Of the 75 students who started French in the third grade in 1955, only 45 completed the full five years. In the course of the last four years these students had to be divided into a regular and a slower "review" group, and both groups were slightly below regular class size.

This problem can continue when FLES groups reach the high school. Diverse levels of language competency produced by different FLES programs may make it necessary for a high school to carry very small sections of these students through several years of the high school (a cumbersome and uneconomical procedure from the administrative point of view). In our own case we have been fortunate thus far. We are having some success filling the ranks with outstanding students who entered the program late and who, in spite of less contact with the language, are (with a little special help) at a high enough level to cope with the more advanced classes. As a result our high-school sections are full.

Such are some of the general problems of staffing and scheduling which face anyone contemplating FLES. Local factors will render some aspects of these same problems different, but probably, if good will and determination are in evidence, will also suggest different practicable local solutions as well.

notes to chapter 2

P. 22. *Staffing a FLES program.* — The following discussions of the general qualifications needed by the foreign-language teacher, though intended primarily for the secondary level, are germane to teachers in FLES: MLA Steering Committee, "Qualifications for Secondary School Teachers of Modern Foreign Languages," *Modern Language Journal*, XXXIX (October, 1955), 290–92; Stephen A. Freeman *et al.*, "The Qualifications of Foreign Language Teachers," *School and Society*, LXXX (November 27, 1954), 165–68; D. Vittorine, "What Makes a

Good Language Teacher?" *Modern Language Journal*, XLI (January, 1957), 48–49; Vincenzo Cioffari, "Factors Involved in Good Modern Language Teaching," *Peabody Journal of Education*, XXXVI (September, 1958), 93–100.

For FLES specifically, see Margaret E. Eaton *et al.*, *Report of the Northeast Conference on Teaching of Foreign Languages* (New York: New York University Press, 1958), pp. 23–26.

P. 22. M. S. Kirch, "Specialist or Classroom Teacher for FLES?" *Modern Language Journal*, XLII (March, 1958), 132–35, sees both as needed at present and agrees with the text that both types have their advantages and disadvantages. J. Kolbert, "Foreign Languages in the Self-Contained Classroom," *ibid.*, (November, 1958), 313–16, on the basis of experience in the Pittsburgh area, argues strongly for the use of the homeroom teacher. Marie-Georgette Steisel, "More FLES for Less," *French Review*, XXXII (February, 1959), 357–61, reports on a program for preparing regular classroom teachers to handle FLES work.

P. 25. *Native speakers.* — Successful use of native speakers in the local community is reported by George W. Brown, "No Trained Teachers for Foreign Languages?" *Nation's Schools*, LV (March, 1955), 53.

P. 25. *Use of high-school or college teachers.* — Agnes Marie Brady, "The Challenge We Face," *University of Kansas Bulletin of Education*, XIII (November, 1958), 1–8, indicates the responsibilities of the teacher about to become involved in a FLES program.

P. 26. Successful use of college students has been reported by several programs: P. M. Gathercole, "Foreign Language Growing in Elementary Schools," *Virginia Journal of Education*, LIII (November, 1959), 13–14; Edith S. Rostos, "A FLES Project and Teacher Training," *French Review*, XXXII (April, 1959), 453–55; Sister Ruth Adelaide, S.C., "The First Door to FLES," *Modern Language Journal*, XLII (April, 1958), 172–74.

3　methods and materials

Certain general principles are usually agreed upon by theorists and participants in FLES.

The audio-lingual approach should be used exclusively, at least in the initial stages of instruction. Views on how long this principle should be pursued vary with different "systems." There are exponents of the purely audio-lingual approach for the entire grade-school period. Our own experience indicates that the introduction of reading during the second year is welcomed by the children and, if properly controlled, can be accomplished without disastrous effect on pronunciation.

Learning should take place by direct association. Objects should be seen as they are named. Actions should be performed as they are designated. This procedure obviously eliminates the "translation" approach to foreign language learning but should be tempered with common sense. Because there is no guaranty that the verbal symbol will be associated accurately with the object or action intended, we have found an occasional word of English a justified insurance against confusion. Similarly, the use of English to describe a background situation or a complicated set of actions is a timesaver. We agree, however, that English should be used very sparingly at either end of the French drill and should not be interspersed with the French.

Mastery of the basic sentence patterns of the foreign language is the paramount objective of instruction, not vocabulary building. Vocabulary is to be introduced incidentally in these basic patterns. Although we agree that this principle is fundamental, nevertheless vocabulary is essential to communication and an analysis of vocabulary content is one familiar way of setting up criteria for achievement.

The classroom atmosphere should be such as to stimulate interest in the foreign language as a functional means of communication rather than as a mere school exercise. This principle suggests that only the foreign language be used during the period of instruction and that out-of-class materials and experiences be provided whenever possible.

As these general tenets are implemented by materials, the following are the major criteria to be used.

Appropriateness of the topic to the interests of the children. Though many topics are known to be of interest to children of a certain age, others are arbitrarily assumed to be interesting (telling time at the third grade level, for instance) and do not really stimulate the anticipated response. It is obvious that interest in the topic or the activity is all-important for the motivation which makes learning possible.

Appropriateness to the mental development of the child. Generally accepted guides and syllabi usually take this factor into consideration. One result may be, however, a minimal expectation: certain elements basic to communication (e.g. common irregular verbs) will be avoided or minimized except in a perfectly controlled situation.

Usefulness of the expressions taught. Most basic guides again concur as to a great many expressions which are natural and useful for the children: greetings, numbers, dates, birthday, foods, animals, etc. We are not sure, however, that *une sucette* should be introduced before *du lait*, for its greater appeal, nor that introduction of the traditional farm animals provides a particularly practical vocabulary for the space age. In selecting vocabulary, a balance between usefulness and interest must be maintained.

Sequential coherence or continuity: a systematic relationship between patterns originally taught and subsequent ones. The development should utilize the old materials as a spring board, through gradual addition, to new materials.

Proper ordering in the presentation of materials: oral modeling of the dialogue, choral repetition, individual response, substitution exercises. If directions for use are not built into the content but instead the order of presentation is left to the discretion of unpracticed teachers, these fundamental techniques may be completely neglected.

Assuming that the materials used conform to these criteria, they can be organized in two different basic patterns.

Situational organization. — Its chief virtue is that it drills the student on materials for situations in which he is now (the classroom) or in which he is likely to be (at the restaurant, at the railroad station) when he uses the foreign language. He has some useful utterances "prefabricated," and what he learns is unified by and attached to the particular situation. One major weakness is that many of the expressions appropriate to one such situation are not usable in another. As a result, drill or review of a given situation tends to demand almost exact repetition of the original lesson, and little of the variation useful in relieving tedium or in testing the ability to change parts of the basic patterns is available.

Topical organization. — This has much the same advantages and disadvantages as the situational. The materials are unified by a single concept, and the student is put in command of the patterns and words necessary for handling a given topic. But likewise, the review of the unit tends to be largely a repetition of the original presentation.

1. *The dialogue approach* — Original presentation by the teacher, followed by dialogue between the teacher and the class or between members of the class. Use of *realia.*

Direct immersion of the student in the foreign languages is the object of this method. Clarification of meaning is achieved through gestures and paraphrasing. Obviously, in many instances to convey the correct and precise meaning becomes very difficult. There is danger of an untoward amount of English intruding into the class period. Dangerous also is the tendency for "improvisation" to result in the introduction of extraneous materials.

2. *The picture approach.* — Materials presented by pictures, drawings, cartoons on the blackboards, etc., followed by questions. Often used with the situational organization.

This approach is seen as minimizing the intrusion of English and as offering a direct psychological bond between the thing pictured and the foreign expression for it. But while most things and some situations are picturable, many concepts either require overly elaborate presentations to convey them through pictures or else are simply not pictographic at all. And even in the simple instances, the danger of confusion is always lurking: the picture of an orange may suggest the kind of fruit, the color, the shape, or something else.

3. *The story approach.* — Story such as "The Three Bears" told in simple vocabulary, accompanied by descriptive

pantomime and/or pictures, followed by questions on the story.

This procedure gives the child an opportunity to hear relatively long connected passages in the foreign language and offers a considerable body of materials on which questions and answers can be based with variation in the patterns. The difficulties rest in the fact that the children will not easily understand all the words they already know in other contexts and that they will not recognize loan-words and cognates because of the difference in pronunciation.

4. *The song and proverb approach.* — Material in the foreign language consists of songs, proverbs, jingles, and games, followed by drill on the patterns and words used and by questions.

Material of this sort gives the student the authentic flavor of the country whose language is studied and contributes to the cultural objectives of a program. Use of this kind of material makes the language class seem very pleasant and makes language learning seem relatively painless. For courses stressing language mastery, however, this approach has limited utility. The patterns and words of this sort of material are often odd or archaic, (though this situation differs somewhat from language to language) and thus are not too useful for elementary communication. Thus the children may seem to be making more progress toward language mastery, (and may feel they are doing so) than is in fact the case.

5. *The dramatization approach.* — The materials used are parts for a play ultimately to be performed by the class.

This teaching device is very effective and is well received by the students. It can bind together many situational or topical units and gives the children the incentive of a clear goal in the near future — being able to present the play to an audience of schoolmates or parents. But the classwork must be certain to involve questions on the material and an interchange of the parts. Otherwise it is possible that, though the children may present the play very fluently and effectively, they may have limited their learning merely to their own role or may have a very sketchy idea of what the dialogue, which they recite so fluently, says precisely.

Our experience has been that all these techniques can be used to advantage and that by varying the approach one can, not only exploit the best that each technique has to offer, but can also avoid the boredom which easily arises in the language class of young children if some one procedure is followed too long. Thus in the third and fourth grades we have used as many as five of these approaches within a single 15-minute period.

These modes of presentation all are becoming enriched and also complicated by the various electronic media as they are being tried in language learning: radio; audio-visual machines (teaching machines, tapes, film-strips synchronized with tapes, sound films, etc.); TV.

With the general rise in interest in audio-visual instruction, an increasing amount of material is becoming available for FLES courses on the various kinds of equipment, and an increasing number of courses use electronic equipment of some sort.

By and large, the following comments are valid for all of them. (1) They are all often used to "spread" good teaching in situations where enough competent teachers are not available or where the expense of hiring them cannot be met. (2) They are frequently used to supplement the "live" teacher in some fashion: to relieve him of some of the strain of continually modeling the correct utterances, to make possible individual instruction by making available multiple models fitted to different levels of progress, to accustom pupils to a variety of voices and intonations, to afford students a better model of the language than the classroom teacher can offer, to vivify and widen the range of cultural materials presented. (3) Apart from the so-called "pinball" effect (or the increase in student interest and attention arising from their general love of gadgets and their eagerness to have electronic devices used in education), there is no special magic in these electronic aids. None of them is better than the materials programed for it or the intelligence with which it is used.

Our own experience with such equipment is very limited for the reason that at the time covered by this report we had very little of it. We ran one interesting, though limited, experiment at the third-grade level. One section was taught by a native speaker. The other was taught by the regular classroom teacher. Her training had consisted of one year of high-school French and two years of college French taught by traditional methods. At the beginning of the year her speech was rated "fair" on the same four-point scale used in rating the pupils.

The two sections were generally comparable at the start of the year. The control group taught by the native speaker was slightly higher in IQ and in ability to mimic French but slightly lower in the rating on probable success in French made by the second-grade teachers.

The native speaker taught the control group completely "live." The classroom teacher was given audio-visual aids, tapes with accompanying slides covering the work of third-grade French. She used these aids with the experimental group for about half of each period; the other half was devoted to "live" drill.

Granting all the difficulties of measurement and especially those of making accurate comparisons between the two sections, at the end of the year pupils in the experimental class had made as much progress, and their pronunciation and aural comprehension were as good, as those of the control group. Though the classroom teacher in the course of the year improved the rating of her own speech from "fair" to "good," nearly a third of her class attained a better pronunciation than she ever achieved. Though the limited nature of this evidence can scarcely be overemphasized, it seems to indicate quite clearly that a judicious use

41

of good audio-visual aides under the supervision of a language specialist can make the regular classroom teacher effective even in a course devoted to language mastery.

Two additional points of caution are worth noting. One is that this teacher, though not a specialist nor even a former "major" in French, was far from wholly untrained. The sense of security as well as the actual knowledge growing out of this fact probably figured in the results. Second, as an elementary teacher skilled in working with this age group and as the teacher working with these same children throughout the school day, she clearly had certain major, though non-linguistic, strengths. Nevertheless, with all due allowances for these and other factors, the performance of the experimental group remains impressive, and the audio-visual aids must receive most of the credit.

There is a plethora of guides and syllabi commercially available for the beginner in French, German and Spanish. These are very adequate as advice to the teacher and seem roughly 80 per cent concomitant as to the expressions introduced. "Workbooks" are beginning to appear for the early stages of instruction. Materials for the third, fourth, and fifth year of instruction are not so readily available at this time but it is hoped that more of them are in the process of being prepared.

Audio-visual aids for beginners are also being introduced on the market and one can rest assured that commercial promotions will soon make available a choice among these materials.

There exists a real shortage of stimulating material for use outside the classroom — few stories have been recorded and practically no books are available where vocabulary and syntax are scaled down to the proficiency and appropriate to the interest level of the children.

Movies also leave much to be desired. Few are appropriate to children, almost none aimed at the beginner's achievement. Poor pictures and bad sound tracks are the rule rather than the exception.

The above remarks are made not to criticize but to indicate the measure in which, especially in the later years of a program, the burden of providing materials falls on the ingenuity of the teacher or program co-ordinator. Such remarks may serve to stimulate commercial materials which could contribute much to the success of FLES in and out of the classroom.

The following is a rough summary of the pattern of instruction provided at the University Elementary School.

The primary objectives, especially for the lower grades are the audio-lingual skills. Reading is then added, at first chiefly as an aid to the aural-oral skills, then with emphasis in its own right. Writing receives relatively little emphasis throughout the program. Until French 5, "grammar" is introduced only to answer questions raised by students in connection with class materials. Cultural materials (chiefly pictorial) are introduced incidentally throughout. Integration with other subjects studied at a given grade is encouraged wherever feasible.

The typical student takes French 1 in Grade III, French 2 in Grade IV and so on. But the transfer students and those who fail to keep up with their group after the first two years take a lower course than that normal for their grade.

A foreign language is not just a collection of words organized by a grammar. The following descriptions give some estimates of the vocabulary burden and a list of some of the chief grammatical features taught to give a rough idea of the kind and amount of material covered each year.

French 1 (Grade III), 15 minutes daily for a total of 41 class hours for the one year

Approach completely oral-aural through choral response, individual questions and answers, dramatizations, song, games, etc. Emphasis on common daily activities at school and home, with classroom situation providing most of the needed *realia*.

Approximately 380 words covering expressions of politeness, numbers, colors, parts of the body, clothing, food. Declarative and interrogative sentences in affirmative and negative. Negative imperative. Verbs generally limited to first person singular and second person plural in present tense.

French 2 (Grade IV), 20 minutes daily for a cumulative total of 96 class hours for the two years

Continuation of oral-aural approach through same devices. Staging of three playlets. Initiation to reading in latter part of year through distribution of scripts of playlets after aural-oral drill on them.

Approximately 350 new words (further items on topics of French 1 and additional units on animals, geography, etc.) Verbs involving all persons of present tense.

French 3 (Grade V), 25 minutes per day, for four days per week for total of 151 class hours for the three years.

Situations extended to include home and neighborhood. Three playlets for oral-aural drill, oral reading and reading comprehension. Training in reading continued with simple materials introduced through aural-oral drill.

380 words relating to the new situations (shopping, furniture, dishes). *Passé composé* introduced and some attempt made to systematize the verb forms met thus far.

Occasional homework assignments made. Children now grouped on basis of achievement in first two years.

French 4 (Grade VI), 25 minutes, four times per week, for a total of 206 class hours for the four years

Greater emphasis on reading. Use of a simple reader as basis for conversation and as material for oral reading and reading comprehension. Reader (Claire A. Roe, *Enfants de Paris*, London: Longman Green & Co., 1954) also unifies and extends cultural materials.

Vocabulary now less rigidly controlled as reading

expands passive vocabulary (e.g. reader contains about 1,000 new words only part of which enter active vocabulary). Imperfect and future tenses introduced.
Regular homework assignments made in reader.

French 5 (Prefreshman year), 50 minutes a day twice a week for cumulative total of 261 class hours in FLES

Effort at systematizing past experience and making transfer to high school through use of a standard high-school grammar. Conversation and reading continued as much as possible.

Little new vocabulary added. About one-half of Theodore Huebener and Marie K. Neuschatz, *Parlez-vous Français* (New York: D. C. Heath & Co., 1958) covered in class.

Two features of this program will possibly seem odd to those familiar with other FLES programs: (1) the early attention given to reading and (2) the introduction of formal grammar.

As for the reading, one extreme position sometimes taken is that foreign language work in the elementary school should be limited to the audio-lingual skills. This view rests on the grounds that the child is best equipped to handle the aural-oral skills — in fact, has a special facility for them which he will later lose — and that this long aural-oral introduction will be the general equivalent of the child's first five or six years of experience with his native tongue. We have no theoretical quarrel with this position. Practically we found it difficult, especially in our situation.

The need for ultimately achieving smooth articulation with high-school work (accompanied by considerable advanced standing accruing from the FLES experience) had always made it obvious that we would eventually need to give our pupils competence in reading normal elementary materials and to pay some slight attention to writing. We also see this transition to reading as serving various additional functions: (1) giving another dimension to FLES instruction (2) offering a chance for review (3) providing a new medium for any students having difficulty with the audio-lingual approach, and (4) enabling us to use some of the standardized tests in evaluating the progress of our students. Nonetheless we hoped for a long period of purely audio-lingual work.

Staffs more skillful than ours, working with children different from ours may well be able to accomplish what we should have liked to do. All we can say is that we could not. We have felt compelled to introduce reading in the form of "oral reading" in the second year, considerably earlier than we had planned. By "oral reading" we mean the reading aloud of materials in normal orthography which have in the preceding months received considerable aural-oral drill. Thus the student presumably comprehends the content of the material and is thoroughly familiar with it in audio-lingual form before he is allowed to "read" the text.

The reasons for the shift in plan were quite simple. For one thing, our students were becoming bored with the completely oral-aural approach. After all, within the limited range of material, how many variations in the general form of the drill are possible, particularly for the slower learners? Moreover, the foreign language class was becoming disassociated from other school subjects because it involved no textbook, no homework, and no written tests. These facts may seem irrelevant, but for children as competitive and inquisitive as ours, the foreign language class began to look like at best a "frill" or an "accomplishment" — something relatively unimportant compared with the serious subjects which were marked by texts, assignments, and batteries of tests. (This situation was not made easier by the fact that some parents were also arriving at this conclusion for these same reasons.) As a result, it was in large part as an effort to clear up this sort of misunderstanding that "reading" in this sense received an earlier introduction than we had planned.

In our estimation the procedure has worked well. The children enjoy it. They are happy to have a "book," which makes French a respectable and serious subject like the others. The introduction of oral reading has also served some of the other purposes we foresaw. It has given a fresh chance to some children, who, for whatever reason, were not responding to the purely aural-oral approach.

As far as we can see, this procedure has had no ill effects on the level of pronunciation and intonation achieved at the end of the aural-oral period, provided certain conditions are maintained. (1) Only materials which have been thoroughly drilled are to be read orally. (2) If there is any doubt about the sufficiency of the drill, the material is re-drilled, or, at a minimum, the teacher reads through the material correctly before the children have an opportunity to mispronounce it on the basis of the spelling. (3) Materials at this stage do not go home where students can practice mispronunciation with each other or with their parents.

In French 3 an attempt is made to enable the children gradually to read aloud words not previously overlearned in aural-oral drill. At first new words are presented with little oral drill. Or when materials are prepared, care is taken that in the alternate reading between the teacher and the class the new words will fall for the first four or five times in the teacher's part and only then appear in the choral response of the class. A further device useful in establishing the correct associations between the sound and the spelling is the list of "key" words for various sounds: *vous* for /u/, *deux* for /ɸ/, and the like. Exercises in building up lists of familiar words under each of the key words has also helped some students achieve a clearer and more accurate pronunciation than they had attained by direct mimicry alone.

During the later part of French 3 a reader is introduced.

47

This provides further work in oral reading, which by now is usually correct except for some apparently perennial pitfalls (e.g., final -tions or final -nt in the third plural of verbs). But the emphasis can now shift to the ability to read for content. The children are not held to a "translation" and analysis into literal meanings is avoided. It is startling to see how, at this stage, the children can render the content into natural, idiomatic English, without any consciousness of the grammatical complexities of the French.

By French 4, correct oral reading is assumed and the emphasis is completely on reading for content.

The second characteristic of our program which may make it appear unusual among FLES programs is our introduction of formal grammatical study. In some respects the reasons for this step were similar to those for the preceding one, although in this case the introduction was delayed until French 5.

The introduction of formal grammar is usually frowned upon by proponents of FLES. It is seen as conflicting with the principles of language learning embodied in the audio-lingual approach and as inappropriate to the stage of mental development which children in the lower grades have reached. We agreed with both these points, but we felt that we had to take certain other considerations into account.

A knowledge of formal grammar is — whether rightly or wrongly is irrelevant here — so commonly demanded that if our pupils lacked it completely certain unfortunate consequences seemed inevitable. For example, our students would eventually be at a considerable disadvantage in high school or college when they took advanced work in more traditional classes with students who had been traditionally trained. Likewise they would labor under a severe handicap, both on the local examinations used for placement and credit in those institutions, and on the various standardized tests and national competitive examinations. Since the competence of our students and the success of our program were to be measured in large part on this basis, we saw no realistic alternative to including a certain amount of grammatical study at some point in our program.

We postponed the introduction of this material until our students were more mature, and until they were becoming increasingly dissatisfied with the many things they knew but could not systematize. Such matters as *le* and *la* or *assis* and *assise* raise questions, of course, even in the first year. Eventually, incidental and limited oral explanations seem to become unsatisfactory to the students as does the attempt to present, as "grammar units," a simple organization of the grammatical points which the students have encountered in their materials. We consequently took the plunge of introducing a standard high-school grammar.

As a pilot group in this undertaking, we used those students who had begun French in the fourth grade at the start of the program in 1955. Since they would have one year less of FLES experience than the third-grade starters, they were already facing the problem of making the transition into regular high school work. In their fourth year, they were given a grammar usually used in the first year of high school and they worked through about half of it. Since the attempt was relatively successful, a second-year grammar was used the following year with those who had started in the third grade and were getting their fifth and last year of FLES experience. Again this experiment worked sufficiently well for us to plan to use these or similar standard texts in French 4 and 5 in the future.

In addition to helping with the problem of enabling the pupils to cope with the usual run of classes and tests, the introduction of formal grammar also served some other functions similar to those performed by the introduction of reading. It offered another approach to some students who had not done well through the audio-lingual approach and thus gave them another opportunity to salvage something from their language experience. Likewise, the use of the grammar gave them a common reference point, helped by giving the "dignity" and reassurance of using a real book, and, of course, offered a framework on which they could systematize the knowledge acquired in a rather scattered fashion during the preceding years.

There were, to be sure, some difficulties attendant upon this effort. One is the fact that use of a standard high-school text with students of this age is difficult because of the standard grammatical nomenclature. Since most schools no longer teach English grammar through the traditional nomenclature at any level, its use in foreign-language instruction is usually an added complication. With younger children the difficulties of the technical vocabulary are very real.

A second complication arises from the fact that the pupils move a little too slowly through such texts. As a result, the slower students especially do not manage in a year to finish what is a year's work in terms of the text. This fact complicates the transfer of these students to other classes in subsequent years. This relatively slow progress is produced by several different factors. One is the terminological difficulty just mentioned. A second factor is the disparity between the vocabulary typically used in FLES materials and that common in the standard high-school texts. Because of this difference the FLES pupils begin such a text with much less of a head start than one might expect them to have.

A third complication in emphasizing grammar is the obvious fact that the time devoted to it is taken from something else, primarily the time given to the audio-lingual skills. Though this change in emphasis does not affect pronunciation, it does affect the progress they could make in fluency. It is our hope, of course, that this temporary setback will justify itself through later increase in command because of this more precise and generalized knowledge.

But, the factors cited earlier which led us to introduce grammatical study are compelling; and despite these difficulties, we feel that the positive features outweighed the negative ones.

notes to chapter 3

P. 36. On the need to use English to insure comprehension, see Blanche A. Price "Feeling and a Foreign Language," *French Review* XXXII (Dec., 1958), 156–59. Nelson Brooks, in the *Report of the Northeast Conference on Teaching of Foreign Languages 1957* (p. 26), presents "no English" as the ideal and lists some restrictions on the emergency use of English.

P. 39. *The song and proverb approach.* — There is a surprising lack of unanimity in the choice of French songs. A survey of some 14 guides and texts provides a list of 113 titles. *Frère Jacques* seems to be the favorite (used by 10 of the 14), closely followed by *Savez-vous planter les choux* and *Alouette* (each used by 9). Other popular choices are *Sur le pont d'Avignon* and *Au clair de la lune* (each used by 8), *Les petites marionettes* (in 7 guides), and *Belle Rosine, Le Coucou,* and *Il était une bergère* (5). Most of the other titles are used by only one text. For example, the *Course of Study for Grades 1-6* published by the Cleveland Public Schools lists some 25 titles unexploited by other guides. It would seem that, apart from the half-dozen favorites, the choice of songs is dictated primarily by personal preference and acquaintance. At least, the fact that *Sur le pont d'Avignon* and *Au clair de la lune* appear in the same number of guides suggests that the linguistic difficulty presented by the songs is not a major criterion in their selection for elementary programs.

There are some reports of "painless" methods of language learning, e.g., Joseph Raymond, "A Child Shall Lead the Way," *California Teachers Association Journal,* LIV (Oct., 1958), 12–13.

The use of games and outdoor sports is advocated by Hugh H. Chapman, "Para poner el Español en el terreno del Juego," *Hispania,* XLIII (March, 1960), 93–96, and Robert E. Loucks's "Teaching Spanish through Games in the Elementary Schools: An Experimental Study," *Hispania,* XLII (May, 1959) 246–47. Scouting and camping have also been utilized: Manuel H. Guerra, "FLES and the Boy and Girl Scouts of America," *Hispania,* XLI (December, 1958), 551–52; Edith Vacheron, "The French Unit in a Girl Scout Camp," *French Review,* XXVIII (January, 1955), 246–51.

All these devices, like the use of plays (Sister Ruth Adelaide, "From French Playlet to FLES," *French Review*, XXXII [December, 1958] 180–81) or pen-pals (Mary Lighthall, "French, 'Par Avion'," *French Review*, XXVIII [Jan., 1955] 264–65) are attempts to provide an artificial yet realistic environment in which the language is spoken, a point given primary stress by J. Donald Bowan, "The Success of FLES," *Hispania*, LXI (September, 1958), 351–53.

The effectiveness of all such devices as compared with more traditional methods, at least as leading to any persistent and extensive achievement, is questioned in articles like John G. Frank's, "Can One Really Learn a Foreign Language at School?" *Modern Language Journal*, XLII (Dec., 1958), 379–81.

P. 40. *Electronic teaching aids.* — For a review of various audio-visual media and their function in the foreign-language classroom, see Chester Babcock and Helen Kwapil, "Audio-Visual Aids in Teaching Foreign Languages," *The National Elementary Principal*, XXXIX (May, 1960), 16–19 or the special issue of *Audio-visual Instruction*, IV (September, 1959), edited by Elton Hocking and Frederick D. Eddy, entitled "What Do We Know about Teaching Modern Foreign Languages?" An annotated bibliography by José Sánchez, "Twenty Years of Modern Language Laboratory," appears in the May, 1959 issue of the *Modern Language Journal*.

The application of audio-visual devices to the teaching of foreign languages is only beginning to reach the elementary-school level, but aids of all sorts are becoming available and being used.

The use of radio is reported in "Detroit Elementary Children Learn German by Radio," *Michigan Educational Journal*, XXXVI (December, 1958), 167.

TV, the newer medium, is getting even greater use. Examples of this sort of instruction are reported by Arthur R. Olson, "Learning Foreign Languages by Television," *National Elementary Principal*, XXXIX (May, 1960), 20–21, Clarissa Sunde, "Spanish Via Television," *Minnesota Journal of Education*, XXXIX (December, 1958), 11–12, Edith Kern, "Language Learning and Television," *Modern Language Journal*, XLIII (October, 1959), 264–65 and her "FLES Testing," *French Review*, XXXII (October, 1959), 45–52. One of the most ambitious of the TV programs directed toward the elementary level is

"Parlons français" under the direction of Earle S. Randall, for the Modern Language Project of the Massachusetts Council for Public Schools. As these notes are written, another major project, the telecasts of the Midwest Program on Airborne Television Instruction (MPATI), has not yet begun.

The use of various other visual aids is reported by Elizabeth Etnire, "The Use of Felt Boards in Teaching Spanish to Small Children," *Hispania*, XLI (December, 1958), 511–12 and James C. Stockton, "A Flashcard Experiment for Teaching Spanish in the Fifth Grade," *Hispania*, XLII (December, 1959), 590–95.

Useful guides to the materials available are the Modern Language Association's *List of Materials for the Teaching of Modern Foreign Languages* (Modern Language Association, 70 Fifth Avenue, New York, N.Y.) and the Council of Chief State School Officers' *Purchase Guide for Programs in Science, Mathematics, and Modern Foreign Languages*, (Boston: Ginn & Co., 1959).

P. 42. *Printed materials.* — Every FLES teacher should be familiar with the MLA's *Teacher's Guides* (For Spanish, German, and French at Grade III and up). These can be obtained from the Educational Publishing Corporation, Darien, Conn. Accompanying records can be purchased through the MLA office, 6 Washington Square, New York, New York.

Many city school systems have also prepared courses of study fitted to their own needs and preferences (e.g., Cleveland, Chicago, St. Louis, New York, San Diego, etc.)

The tendency to organize a unique local program is apparently very strong. The values of fitting local needs and local situations cannot be denied, but the danger of needless duplication of effort should be kept clearly in view. Then too, the enormous diversity among present programs makes communication and comparison very difficult. Those undertaking the construction of still another program should at least be familiar with existing materials and know something about prevailing view and practices. Articles like Julian Harris' "Let's Take the Guess Work out of the Teaching of Foreign Languages in the Elementary School," *French Review*, XXVIII (February, 1955), 410–18, provide useful orientation. Lists of existing guides and texts may be found in Marjorie Johnston and Ilo Remer, *References on Foreign Languages in the Elementary School*, ("U.S. Department of Health, Education and Welfare," Circular

No. 495 [Revised], [Washington: U.S. Office of Education, 1959]), and the MLA *Materials List.*

P. 42. *Workbooks.* — Catherine Bill Osborn's "Necessary Tools for FLES," *French Review,* XXXI (April, 1958), 438–39 speaks to the use of a workbook as a means of compensating for slackening student interest after the first year's exposure. This position is challenged by Robert Brooks in a "Letter to the Editor," *French Review,* XXXII (October, 1958), 70.

Since workbooks keep appearing, a number of teachers apparently find them useful as a supplement to audio-lingual presentation. Thus Margit McRae offers *Mi Cuaderno de Español* (Boston: Houghton Mifflin Co., 1959) to accompany her *Spanish in the Grades.* A more sequential and comprehensive series is the *Elementary French Series* of Mother Raymond de Jesus, F.S.E. and Claude L. Bourcier (Boston: Allyn and Bacon, 1960). The four volumes of this series (*Bonjour, Venez voir, Je sais lire,* and *Je lis avec joie*) gradually involve the pupils in all the language skills.

P. 42. *Material for use outside the classroom.* — Supplementary readers constitute a controversial issue since they involve the larger question of when, if ever, FLES pupils should be exposed to the written word. The discussion takes on a less doctrinaire tone, however, if we acknowledge the fact that many children do like books and that pupils and their families do own, look at, and buy books in the foreign language and that they will probably continue to do so in spite of any ukase of a FLES program to the contrary. It is unfortunate that this interest, which could provide additional contact with the language and which could be used as a source of motivation, soon aborts and results in frustration because of the discrepancy between the topical interest of the books and their level of language difficulty. In our experience, children's books in French (with few exceptions like Edith Vacheron's *Voici Henri* [New York: Scribners Sons, 1959]) are inaccessible to FLES students. That hosts of such books are available in bookstores and are constantly cited in guides and lists of materials implies a wealth of material which is purely illusory.

P. 45. The controversial questions of when and why introduce reading and grammar are discussed at greater length by Vincenzo Cioffari in "Grammar — Beware!" *Modern Language*

Journal, XLII (October, 1958), 284–87; James H. Grew *et al.,* in the *Report of the Northeast Conference on Teaching of Foreign Languages* (New York: New York University Press, 1957), pp. 25–35; and Filomena C. Peloro, *ibid.* (1959), pp. 35–41.

4 selection, sectioning, and special help

Who should be enrolled in FLES courses? Will all children benefit from the study of foreign languages? Or if certain students are to be selected for the program, on what basis are they to be selected? And once students are in the program, what devices can be used to cope with the inevitable errors in selection or with the (even more inevitable) different rates of individual progress?

The elementary school curriculum is not marked by elective subjects. It is usually regarded as the scene of the "common learnings," those basic knowledges and skills which all children in our society are likely to need and that broad range of experiences to which all children should be exposed in order for each of them to discover his particular interests and talents. But the extended development of those special interests or the satisfaction of those special needs is usually left for secondary education.

There have been exceptions to this general mode of procedure. Some school systems have had a fairly long tradition that children in the upper grades or junior high school who were planning an "academic" secondary program could begin the elective study of such subjects as algebra and Latin. Thus foreign language has some tradition as an elective in the elementary school, at least in the upper grades. This practice is also related to our current common phenomenon, the "enrichment" program offered in many schools for the more able students. Many FLES courses have been parts of such programs.

The status of foreign language in these latter programs depends in large part, of course, on the particular kind of language work offered and the reasons for including it in the enrichment program. We have doubts about some of the reasons often followed. If foreign languages are seen as simply an extra subject for which abler students have the time because they complete their other work more easily and rapidly than the bulk of the children, then almost any kind of course can serve as an additional experience. But sometimes foreign languages are considered to be particularly suited to "bright" children, who are usually so classified on the basis of IQ, past scholastic achievement, or both. But neither of these criteria is a very satisfactory predictor of attainment in elementary language mastery, and the assumption that only "bright" children (thus defined) will do well in language learning simply is not true, as we shall see in a moment.

Since the University Elementary School has a selective admissions policy, the curriculum as a whole might well be considered an enriched program for able students. But since every child in the third grade and above was enrolled in a language class, our problems were those met when foreign languages are made part of the regular curriculum and offered to all students.

Many of these complications stem from a fundamental characteristic of language study if the aim is mastery of a language. Foreign language study is homogeneous and hence cumulative. Other parts of the elementary curriculum are often made up of elements of rather varied sorts. The child who is unsuccessful or disinterested in one part may later get a change of scene and something of a chance to start fresh. In science, for example, the child who is bored with magnets may come alive when plants or animals are studied, and his lack of knowledge about magnetic forces will not penalize him in his study of these later topics. The student who mishandles fractions has another chance when he reaches decimals. Similarly with many elements in the social studies and the rest of the curriculum, the type of content and the kind of activity connected with it change fairly markedly from time to time.

But the study of a foreign language for the sake of gaining a command of it remains pretty much the same. Something wholly new is never going to become the object of primary focus. And though some areas of difficulty can be cleared up in the course of time, the student can never write off a semester or a year of lack of progress on the ground that sooner or later he will come to an area of the language where the knowledge and skills which he earlier failed to acquire will be unimportant or irrelevant. On the contrary, the difficulties and confusions tend to become compounded. The parallel, of course, is with English and the language arts where the child with a reading difficulty, for example, merely gets deeper and deeper into trouble in more and more areas as he progresses through the elementary school.

If then we are going to offer foreign languages to all students in the elementary curriculum and ask them to continue in the program for three to eight years, we must face the question whether all children are capable of acquiring an elementary command of the foreign language that will justify the time and effort. If the student gets off on the wrong foot, how can he be got back in step? If he has no interest or ability, what can be done with him? Is he simply doomed for the duration of the program?

Considerations of whether all children are competent are often confused by overemphasis on a false analogy with the child's learning of his native language. To be sure, all children in France learn French at an early age. But the interests, opportunities, motivations, and pressures which are involved in a child's learning of his mother tongue are quite different from those operating in the necessarily artificial situation in which he studies a foreign language for two or three hours per week as one among several school subjects. And not all children, even in learning their native language, reach the same level of proficiency, and certainly they do not all reach any one level at the same time. In our own schools the ubiquity of the speech clinician, the reading clinician, the remedial-reading class, demonstrates quite convincingly that not all children master even the native language with ease and at the same rate. To assume, therefore, that because all young children get some control of their native language at some point in their early years, all young children will be proficient in studying foreign language as a school subject (provided only that it is taught to them early enough) is to strain credulity and to ignore a good many facts.

Our own experience has revealed each year a tremendous range in achievement between students in the same grade, though they used the same materials and were often taught by the same teacher. This spread occurs in all areas — pronunciation, fluency, aural comprehension, and the rest. To illustrate in merely one area, a 23-item test of aural comprehension administered to several first-year classes in various years shows ranges of 5-22, 8-22, and 7-23. Each year some students had mastered nearly all the materials sampled by this test; some of their classmates could handle only about a third of it or less.

Furthermore, these differences persist and tend to increase in magnitude. Thus, again merely to take one example from the large chart on p. 118, one child (Student A) made a score of 42 on the 45-item test of aural comprehension administered in the first year of the program, while Student Z scored only 5. Five years later, on the Co-operative Listening Test, Student A's percentile rank was 87; Z's was 1.

These differences persist in spite of serious, direct efforts of various kinds to reduce them. During the second year of the program considerable emphasis was given to review in an effort to close the gap between the better and the poorer students already evident after one year's work. This procedure helped the very poorest students somewhat, but it was much less effective with those less near the bottom. In any case, the chasm was far from bridged.

Further evidence of this same sort is available from the results of the third year (pp. 102ff.). There Section B devoted much time to reviewing the materials of the preceding two years, but 14 per cent of these students did no better at the end of the third year than they had done at the end of the second. The poorest third-year students were placed in Section C and began the first-year materials again. Five members of this group managed to do even worse at the end of the third year than they had done at the end of the second.

These facts have indicated to us very clearly that some children do not have whatever it takes (be it aptitude, readiness, motivation, or maturity) to be able to study a foreign language in a course aiming at linguistic mastery, and that these students show little or no improvement in the course of time (or at least we were unable to effect much improvement). This situation seems likely to prevail in all FLES programs of similar type and aims. To avoid the obvious difficulties inherent in this situation several courses of action seem possible.

Selection.—One way out is to determine in advance those students not likely to benefit from the work and to plan another sort of program for them. If one could determine in advance who these students were, this alternative could take several different forms.

This group could be enrolled in some completely different subject. This possibility seems plausible in the sense that certainly the pupils' time could be better employed elsewhere, but it involves some difficulties. First is the question of what precisely this work should be. For some, the prescription often seems obvious. For example, those having difficulty in mastering the reading and writing of English might well spend the additional time on those skills. If all members of the group can profit from some single activity of this sort, this solution is easy and good. But in our classes the group concerned often constituted a "mixed bag." Thus while some of them could obviously profit from additional work in one area, for others individual treatment seemed most appropriate, but few schools have the flexibility of staff and schedule to provide such treatment.

Another variety of alternative which could meet some of these difficulties is a FLES class which minimizes the linguistic skills and gives greater emphasis to the social and cultural objectives. Thus all these children as a group could gain a widened experience with a foreign land and people, could achieve some of the objectives of language study, and yet would avoid the deadening experience of attempting to master skills for which they have either no ability or no inclination. There is, of course, the difficulty that, in our school at least, the non-linguistic class might be regarded as a "dummy" or "retarded" section, an implication which neither pupils nor parents would suffer gladly. But we have no data on the probable effectiveness of this solution since for our purposes we kept our classes pointed toward the linguistic goals.

The chief difficulty with selection is that we have found it impossible. Since this was a problem which interested us from the outset, we tested diverse kinds of data for its ability to predict success in our program.

The newest and best of the prognostic tests, the Carroll and Sapon test, was not intended for second graders, and the older tests suffer the same shortcoming. But even at the levels for which they are intended, prognostic tests rarely predict individual performance with sufficient accuracy for them to be used in situations of this sort.

The IQ proved to be of very limited usefulness. This result might well have been expected since the IQ usually does not correlate highly even with reading ability in English at the third-grade level. At any rate, for this grade we obtained correlations ranging between .28 and .32, far too low to select individuals with any confidence.

To be sure, the school's selective admissions policy tends to produce a truncated distribution of IQ's. Distributions of the IQ's are made and local percentiles computed every few years, though they vary little from one time to the next. This was the distribution current at the time of our experiment:

P90 155
P75 144
P50 132
P25 122
P10 113
M 130.3
S.D. 18
Range 85-179

P . . . percentile; M . . . median; S.D. . . . standard deviation.

Granted that a distribution of this sort will tend to produce unusually low correlations with IQ, we are generally dubious of the effectiveness of the IQ as a predictor of achievement in foreign-language work.

The Wepman Auditory Discrimination Test had often been found by the school to be a useful predictive and diagnostic instrument for those having difficulty with reading at this grade level. Administering this test in 1960, we obtained a correlation of only .12 between it and achievement in French.

On the theory that the Seashore Musical Aptitude test might be useful in regard to some elements of the audio-lingual skills in the foreign language, we used it early in the experiment. The total score produced an r of .37, but the various parts did no better than the total.

As for correlation of French with other academic areas, the Chicago Developmental Reading Test is used regularly by the school. The $r's$ obtained for it ran from .25 to .52. Another test regularly used by the school, the Iowa Every Pupil Arithmetic Test, gave correlations of about the same magnitude.

In sum, these tests probably measure some of the specific factors involved in language mastery, but any one of them has very limited value in predicting success in the first year's work. More complicated techniques involving multiple regression or factor analysis would probably have shed considerable theoretical light on this problem had the testing time been available to secure all these data for some one group. But even for research purposes we felt we could not justify stealing so much of the limited class time, since even interesting findings from that investigation would probably not have offered a practical solution to our problem within the limitations of the situation.

The preceding data seemed to indicate quite clearly that we should not be able to select students in advance of the course by using the kind of objective measures just examined. Another (and perhaps the only other) possibility was to use subjective estimates of the pupils' probable success. For this purpose the best placed and most skilled observers seemed to us to be the home-room teachers who had taught these children for a year before they began French. In the late spring of 1959, consequently we asked the second-grade home-room teachers to rate their pupils on several scales covering two general areas. One of these was the area of academic achievement, with specific ratings on general academic achievement, oral reading ability, and ability to verbalize. The second area involved more general personality characteristics, attitudes, and habits: general emotional attitudes, attitudes toward school work, self-control, general work habits, and attentiveness. We also asked them to indicate any special problems which each student had. In short, we asked these teachers to indicate in terms of academic performance "good students" and "bad students" and "nice kids" and "difficult kids" regardless of academic performance.

The teachers had obviously selected one group of second graders as outstanding, rating them excellent both in academic performance and in attitudes and habits. Of the seventy-nine pupils then in Grade II, nineteen fell into this group. At the other end of the scale a contrasting "poor" group was much less apparent. This fact may reflect either the selective admissions policy of the school or the eternal optimism and kindliness of primary-grade teachers. Whatever the reason, few ratings of "poor" were assigned. One boy received that rating in both areas, and two other students received it in one, the area of attitudes and habits. Thus even if a rating of "poor" in one of the general areas proved to be a perfect predictor of difficulty with French in the next grade, we could thus rule out only three students. Yet we knew from previous experience that the probabilities were that eight to ten of the pupils actually would have sufficient difficulty to make it desirable to detect them in advance or very early in the course. Consequently, if we were to test the predictive value of these ratings it would be necessary to increase the size of our "poor" group.

To get this enlargement we added the three students who received the rating "fair" in both areas, and then the eleven who received it in one. Thus we got a "poor" group of seventeen students, which is still slightly smaller than the nineteen clearly chosen as excellent in all respects. But since the remaining ratings are "good" or "excellent," we could not further increase the size of this low group. But in view of the predominance of the higher ratings, we felt it justifiable to count even the "fair" ratings as clues to difficulty of some sort on the part of students receiving them.

On the scale of actual performance in French the next year, nine of the fifty pupils were outstanding and eleven were having sufficient difficulty to make them typical examples of the kind of case we should like to be able to detect in advance. Several questions can, therefore, be asked. How well did the ratings predict subsequent success in the first year of French? But more important from the standpoint of selection, "How well did these judgments predict failure?" and "Did negative judgment ever predict failure inaccurately so that a student who actually proved successful would have been prevented or advised from taking French if we had used the judgments as the criterion of selection?"

Prediction of success should have been fairly easy. Since we are concerned with only the nine top performers and since nineteen students had been rated excellent, sheer weight of numbers should increase the probability that all nine should have come from the nineteen rated excellent. Seven in fact did. But the eighth member of the group of top performers, though rated "excellent" in academic achievement, was marked only "good" in the area of attitudes and habits, and the ninth member had been rated merely "fair" in both areas (one of the six lowest ratings in the entire second grade). Thus the rating did not pick out unerringly those students who would do well, and, in fact, had we used them for selection, would have prevented one of the best performers from taking the course.

In examining the ability of the ratings to predict the lower end of the achievement distribution, we find a complication in the fact that three of the children with low ratings either left the school at the end of the second grade or in the third grade were absent for one or more of the tests which make up the performance scale. Thus their cases drop out of any consideration of the accuracy of the prediction. Conversely, two of the actual poor performers were children who entered the school at the third grade and for whom no ratings from the second grade are available. Of the remaining nine poor performers for whom ratings exist, the ratings accurately predicted the failure of six. One other poor performer is a boy whose home-room teacher in second grade passed over his name without rating or comment, whether because of a clerical error on her part or something more, we cannot say. In any case, the other two poor performers come from high on the rating list. One was rated "excellent" on both academic achievement and attitudes; the other was rated "good" on the first and "excellent" on the second. And eight children with low ratings are performing well enough. For example, the boy with the lowest rating of all ("poor" on both counts) stands just below the median of his class on performance.

Thus far we have been dealing with the two general ratings, the one in regard to academic achievement and the other in regard to general attitudes and habits. But if we look at the specific components of those ratings, the data are no more enlightening. No single element or pair of them appears more predictive than the general rating in the area of which it is a part.

Much the same is true of the specific problems which the second-grade teachers noted concerning certain students. The pupil marked "retarded in the language arts" is close to the middle of the class on the scale of performance. The two children who are said "not to hear sounds correctly" are doing even better than that average performance. On the other hand, one child who was said to have "speech and other problems" did in fact do poorly.

In short, ratings are very much like the other indexes. They tell us something. They do correlate positively with actual performance. But the correlation is of such a low order that the ratings should not be used for selection in individual cases. Thus, had we used them with this class we would have properly eliminated in advance about half our poorest students. But simultaneously we would have deprived of the opportunity to learn French an even larger number of students who actually demonstrated their ability to profit from the course.

The unsuccessful student is so challenging and vexing a problem — certainly for a course like ours — that it seems worthwhile to examine briefly a few of these individual cases. These will illustrate in rather typical fashion, not merely the problem of prediction, but also the equally important one of remediation. If we cannot discover these cases in advance (and we, at least, are prepared to confess we cannot), there is still the problem of discovering the cause of the difficulty and doing something about it once language study is begun. The cases, merely taken in order from the bottom of the achievement distribution for this class, exhibit a fair sample of the difficulties.

Our lowest achiever is a boy with an IQ of 130. This is not extremely high for our children, but clearly he is not feeble-minded. In the third grade his score in reading was well above fourth-grade level. Nonetheless, his second-grade teacher noted that he was "negative," and rated his general attitude and his self-control as only "fair" though she classed him "good" in many categories, including that of general academic achievement. A very different suggestion is the comment of his French teacher; "A very shy boy; will not speak up unless absolutely certain of his answers." If he is shy, then he is likely to find the audio-lingual approach uncongenial and thus his performance in French might well be out of line with his achievement in reading and elsewhere. But whether negativism or shyness is the cause, clearly, emotional difficulties rather than lack of intellectual capacity are the cause of his relatively poor performance in French as compared with other subjects. Whether the source of the trouble can be discovered and worked within the language class is another matter.

The next lowest boy shows a similar, but far from identical pattern. His IQ is good enough (137), and he too read at a grade in advance of his actual level. But his home-room teacher in the second grade marked him only "fair" on all the emotional and attitudinal scales (the lowest ranking she gave to any child in her homeroom) though she rated him "good" in the academic area. In this case the comment of the French teacher possibly says much the same thing as did the rating: "stubbornly refuses to participate." Here again the trouble is apparently a matter of attitude and habit rather than one of ability, but quite clearly a different set from those in the preceding case.

The next lowest child is a girl who has an IQ of 124 and also reads at a level a year above her grade. But her second-grade teacher rated her poor on work habits, attentiveness, self-control, and noted that "she wants to be a leader in all the wrong ways." The comment of her French teacher was: "she does not apply herself." Since the second-grade teacher rated her academic performance also as only "fair," perhaps we have here another student whose attitudes, habits, and perhaps interests are making the student a problem in the French class, and elsewhere.

Our next case may be like the first one we examined above, but perhaps not. This is a girl with an IQ of 123 with a reading placement two full years in advance of her grade. Her second-grade teacher rated her as "excellent" on nearly all counts, but added the qualification that she was "verbally reticent" and put her ability to verbalize at only "fair." These comments might lead us to suspect that she is another case like the first one — a shy child who finds the audio-lingual procedure uncongenial and hence performs in French at a level below that which she achieves elsewhere. But, astonishingly enough, the following year she was classed by her French teacher among those "who participate actively in class, extremely verbal, and quick." Possibly the only way to integrate these diverse comments is to suggest that she changed. But if she has changed in this respect, then one wonders why her performance is not better. But whatever the cause of her difficulty, it is not obvious, and diagnosis and remediation of it will be neither easy nor quick.

The next and last case we shall consider briefly is different but no more simple. Though this boy has an IQ of 128, he had the lowest reading placement of any child in the class, reading below his grade level. Even in the second grade his home-room teacher rated his academic achievement as "bad," adding a new fifth point of her own below "poor" on the four-point scale, apparently to take care of this particular case. On most of the other scales she indicates that his behavior fluctuates almost daily, swinging from "excellent" to "poor." Most interesting, however, is her further comment, offered apparently as a partial explanation of his lack of scholastic achievement despite his IQ: "He tries to please rather than learn." Against the background of this comment, the judgment of his French teacher the next year is striking. She says, "low capacity," and names him among a group exhibiting "general lack of attention, disinterest, and non-concern for classroom activity." Since an IQ of 128 is hardly a low capacity, even for our school, that capacity is clearly not being utilized; and perhaps the difficult child is merely being misperceived as the stupid child. Be that as it may, the child who was eager to please in the second grade has, in the third grade, become a difficult child, at least in the French class. This kind of change can, of course, easily happen. The pupil who loses out moves fairly regularly through the stages of being withdrawn, angry, and then openly disruptive.

The problems here are apparent. One of our best performers is a child with an IQ of 177. His second-grade teacher, after rating him excellent in everything, added "A wonderful child." But a still better performer, one of our top three, is a boy with lower ratings and an IQ of 100, one of the lowest in the class and the school. Not all the children with high IQ's and high ratings are successful, and the boy with the lowest ratings, who is average in the grade, and who is noted as having psychological problems, does almost as well as the average.

Many of our failing students, as we have seen in the few cases outlined, seem to have the wrong attitudes, to be inattentive, etc. For most specific cases of failure it is probably possible to offer some fairly plausible reason for it. The child is lazy, uninterested in school work, has personality problems. The difficulty is that other students bearing those same labels, succeed fairly well. And labeling is not the same as curing.

Removal. — Since various devices do not adequately predict success in the first year's work, another possibility is to use that performance as the criterion itself and to plan other programs for those pupils doing poorly at the end of the first year. As usual in the prognosis of achievement in foreign-language study, a sample of actual work in the course is the best predictor. With so large a sample of the first year's work, the prognosis is fairly decisive. Few students in later years depart from the prediction possible at the end of the first — and this despite some special efforts to improve the standing of these students in the second and third year, as we have already seen.

The alternative programs for students removed from the program would be, of course, the same as those possible for students not allowed to enter the program if some satisfactory basis for selection could be found. And again probably the easiest alternative is the foreign language course with different (and preferably, less demanding) objectives. But removal involves some difficulties which selection does not. For one, ejection from the program is even harder on pupils and parents than is initial exclusion, for at this point the parent thinks he has some evidence of his own about the child's ability. Unless the parent is fairly competent himself, he is likely to feel that the ability to rattle off a few routine phrases bespeaks much better progress and a much greater command than is in fact the case. (We have had cases where our poorest students sounded very impressive to parents who know little or no French.) If the change in the type of course to which a student is exposed is made without informing the child and his parents of the value and reasons for the shift, the psychological difficulties are avoided, but then confusion sets in. The parents and the child think he is still acquiring a mastery of the language, and they are likely to be the group most surprised if the child does not win advanced standing in high school because of his FLES experience. A fourth difficulty, if the child is removed from a language program to some other type of course, is that he seems to have "failed French." In most elementary schools, students may be marked as deficient in subjects like math or science but they still continue the study of them in the next grade and the new teacher attempts to remedy the deficiency. To have to drop a subject because of lack of success in it is something of an anomaly in the practice of most elementary schools. (Here the heterogeneity of many other subjects makes a difference, in contrast to the cumulative nature of foreign language work.)

Because of our situation and purposes, we did not use either selection or removal, but sectioning.

Sectioning. — Many of the familiar objections to grouping students on the basis of ability do not seem appropriate in relation to a course which stresses the language skills. Some light may be thrown on the general situation by considering other sorts of skills. The better tennis player, for example, does not improve his game by always playing with a dub. Nor does the dub improve by playing with the superior player unless the latter slows down his efforts enormously, becoming only something little better than the tyro. Otherwise the inexpert player would probably never get his racket on the ball. If attaining greater skill and enjoying the full use of it are the objects of the game, then both sorts of players do better when each is more evenly matched.

To some extent an analogous state of affairs prevails in

71

the language class where the emphasis is on mastering the language skills. The better students, no longer held back by the less able, do forge ahead. (This further widening of the initial gap between the two groups makes them still more distinct and can present long-term problems in grouping and scheduling.)

The effect on the poorer sections is, however, less salubrious. One important cause of this result is the fact that these poorer sections do not contain merely the less skilled student; they contain the uninterested, the troubled, etc. In terms of the earlier analogy, it is as if the poorer tennis players were always matched, not only with their like but also with people who didn't like to play tennis or were severely crippled. As a consequence, in our experience at least, these slower sections are usually marked by an apathy and resistance which are difficult, if not impossible, to counteract. If, of course, these slower sections contained only students who were interested and well adjusted but were merely less able, then the slower sections might be effective. These groups would merely proceed at a slower pace and with other adjustments suited to their capacities. But then, if the difficult students were removed, the need for sectioning by ability might be considerably less. It is the presence of the apathetic and disturbed student which is the chief brake on the progress of the group.

In short, we see our experience with sectioning as another bit of evidence favoring a policy of providing some other sort of experience for that 10 per cent of the students who can make little or no progress in a course concentrating on mastering the language skills.

Special help. — Another device we have tried in coping with the general problem of the poorer student is that of special help. This attempt can take a number of forms: remedial classes after school, special materials for use at home, or devotion of regular class time to various remedial measures, such as review intended primarily for the lowest quarter of the class.

In the schedule of our school (and, we suspect, that of most other elementary schools), remedial work on a regular basis could be provided only outside the already crowded school day. In 1957–58 and 1958–59 we tried this device in a major, organized fashion and met with difficulty on two counts. First, the child who has failed to grasp the material during the regular class hour is likely to become merely bored and irritated by further drill. At the early elementary stages, the scope of the material is so limited that only the utmost ingenuity can provide enough variation in materials and procedures to stave off boredom in the necessary drill. Adding additional remedial classes over the same material exacerbates this difficulty. Furthermore, relatively few students have difficulty because too much was presented too fast in the regular class hour, the kind of trouble for which additional remedial work is an effective remedy. More commonly the trouble of these students stems from some difficulty which further teaching in itself simply does not reach — lack of interest, personality problems, etc.

A second difficulty with the use of after-school time is that it is seen by the child as an encroachment on his playtime and by the parent as an unwelcome disruption of the schedule of such after-school activities as catching the school bus home, taking a music lesson, or going to the dentist. Though some students benefited from these classes, the effectiveness of scheduled remedial or review classes after school was considerably less than we had hoped.

Since we did not then have the facilities of a language laboratory which could be used by students on an unscheduled basis before or after school, we have no knowledge on this point. But passing over the technical difficulties and the problems inherent in the use of such equipment by nine- and ten-year olds, we would point out that even such facilities are not likely to solve the most difficult parts of the problem, the disinterested or the troubled or the troublesome student.

A second variety of remedial work is that possible at home. Parents whose children are having difficulty frequently are willing to do anything they can to help. Sometimes, without consulting the teacher, parents buy one or more of the recorded language courses in order to give their child additional practice. And when one or both parents know a little of the language, they often attempt tutoring the child, with or without help from the school.

Certainly further work at home does extend the student's opportunity for contact with the foreign language and for further drill. But for our type of program at least, there is considerable difficulty and even some danger in this sort of co-operation. Only rarely does a parent speak the language well enough to serve as a good model or competent drill-master. If he is not, the student merely practices his existing bad habits or acquires new ones from the parent. The recorded language courses usually present good models, but they cover somewhat different materials. As a result, they make relatively little contribution to the student's work in the course because they actually tend to double the mass of material with which the student is trying to deal. Selecting and preparing materials (based on our own course) which could be used at home to advantage by the student alone or by student with parental help is a complicated problem to which we and most other programs have been able to give little attention. Providing recordings is an expensive and complicated process. Providing written materials which are likely to help rather than hinder has been possible only on a very small scale.

A third variety of special assistance is to devote the regular class hour to what is essentially remedial work. In the second year of our program, rather than use sectioning on the basis of achievement, we devoted a considerable portion of the class time to review. This procedure had the advantage of avoiding any stigma arising from ability grouping and the problems of remediation after school or at home. And some of the children did benefit from this extended review. But not all of them did, and there was a price paid in the progress of the upper and middle groups who did not need this slow and intensive work and who profited little from it.

In summary, then, selection, sectioning, and remediation are all primarily devices for dealing with the "poor" student. But students are "poor" for several, quite distinct kinds of reason. There is the student who is "poor" only relative to those more competent in the language skills. For this kind of poor student all the devices mentioned have considerable effectiveness. To be able to go at a slower pace, to have additional time for practice, to have extra, thoroughgoing review — all help the student who is poor in this sense. This "poorness" arising from differences in capacity and different rates of development causes some difficulty. But it can be dealt with and is not disheartening to the teacher or particularly disturbing to the rest of the class.

The major difficulty is the student who is "poor" for various other reasons. He may simply not be interested in learning French. Some enthusiasts might hold that every student should be interested in learning French and can be made so, provided only the teacher is creative enough to find the right way. As we have suggested, if "learning French" is interpreted with considerable laxity to include "studying something about France and the French," then the statement gains considerable plausibility. Students uninterested in mastering the French language may quite possibly be interested in other aspects of French life and civilization. But when "learning French" is narrowly construed to mean "acquiring a mastery of the French language," the scope for creative ingenuity is considerably reduced. And the limitations of regular class instruction in fairly sizable groups curtails still further what is feasible. Thus we end by having some students who, rightly or wrongly, are just not eager to learn a foreign language.

Then there are the other students "poor" because of immaturity, personality problems, family problems, etc. Often the students constitute examples of academic, social, or disciplinary difficulty familiar to the entire faculty. The problems involved are usually inappropriate and too big for the language teacher and the language class. The school psychologist or social worker or outside therapists and agencies are those capable of working with the true source of the trouble and often they do much to help.

Meanwhile the language class must probably bear its share of these burdens just as do other classes in the school, provided these children are no worse off in the language class than they are in any other. Here we can only suggest that perhaps the cumulative nature of language study may make a difference. On the students' side, their possibilities of eventual success are continually diminished, and the pupils are merely confirmed in their role of misfit or outcast. On the side of their classmates, poor students of this sort are a continual and ever increasing drag on the progress of the rest of the group. In less cumulative studies the price may possibly be less high. If, of course, there is nothing better for these students than language work or if they are no worse off in the language class than they are in any other, then they will have to remain. But we think both those points demand scrutiny.

notes to chapter 4

P. 56. *Selection.* — Some discussions of selectivity hinge on whether it is necessary; others raise the issue of whether it is democratic: e.g., Emile B. De Sauzé and Lurline V. Simpson, "Selection vs. Free Registration in French Classes," *French Review*, XXXI (April, 1958) 427–30, Agnes M. Brady, "The Life Cycle of an Idea," *Hispania*, XXXVII (March, 1954), 68–70.

Selection on the basis of achievement during a trial period is suggested by Georgina Hicks, "Findings of the FLES Program in Muncie, Indiana," *French Review*, XXXII (October, 1958), 62–65.

The need for selection as at least a temporary expedient necessary because of the shortage of competent teachers for FLES is suggested by Elizabeth R. Ratté, "Foreign Languages for Some or for all?" *Modern Language Journal*, XLI (November, 1957), 355.

5   the starting point for instruction

In most discussion, three general grade-levels are seen as the likely points at which FLES programs can begin: nursery school, kindergarten, Grade I; Grades III and IV; grades VII and VIII. Each possibility has its own general theoretical advantages and disadvantages, and the feasibility of any one of them is further conditioned by factors in the local situation.

The desirability of the preschool or first-grade start rests primarily on two principles: "The sooner the better" and "The earlier the longer." At this age children's vocal and mental habits are still extremely flexible. The exclusively oral-aural emphasis seems quite natural to them because it is the only kind of activity they are familiar with in any language. Songs and games form a large part of the day's schedule at these levels, and there is no reason why these cannot be in the foreign language. Thus foreign language becomes part of the day's regular activities, and the children can be said to grow into it naturally. Foreign language is not a subject, but simply something one does. And obviously the earlier the beginning, the longer the program which is possible in the elementary-school years.

These are all great advantages, but before they and the accompanying disadvantages can be accurately assessed, what is meant by "program" (when one speaks of "foreign language program" at this level) must be clear. Since the rise of the FLES movement, many teachers who have some mastery of a foreign language have felt freer to introduce songs and games in that language. This activity, however, is not regarded as the first stage in a continuous program of foreign language instruction. It is seen merely as a good way of adding variety and interest to the children's activity. Thus the kindergarten teacher may have majored in French, the first-grade teacher comes from a German family, and so on. Each introduces whatever seems interesting and appropriate in connection with the other work of the grade. Creative teachers have always done this sort of thing, and certainly we have no objection — quite the contrary — to it. But our interest here is in a continuous program in a single language, extending over two (and preferably, considerably more) years. For this sort of program the advantages cited earlier still obtain. But obtaining them in a continuous program involves certain problems.

Some of these problems concern the teacher. In nursery school and kindergarten the use of a special teacher of foreign language is probably impossible. Even those schools which use special teachers for various subjects at higher grades usually at this level follow the principle of the self-contained classroom on the grounds that young children should not be asked to relate to a large number of people. The problems of using the classroom teacher (already discussed in chapter 2) then appear: getting teachers who are adequate models, getting a succession of them who are all adequate in the same language, etc. As was indicated earlier, audio-visual aids can be of great use here when enough of them are available. Thus recordings of songs, of the words necessary to play the various games, and the like can give the pupils a better model than the teacher may be able to offer. Other possible disadvantages were mentioned in chapter 1.

Grades III and IV find the children already introduced to the reading and writing of their native language and more mature. They are capable of better attention and more accustomed to school life, but their motor and mental habits are still flexible. And even this later start still leaves a span of five or six years for the study of foreign language in the elementary school. Since this is the level at which our own program began, we shall postpone the discussion of the attendant problems to the account of our own experience later in this chapter.

Courses beginning at grades VII and VIII seem to be fairly common. Two causes tend to make this period popular. The first has already been mentioned earlier, the tradition of offering a foreign language, at least as an elective for abler students, along with algebra and other "high-school" subjects. As a result, many of the problems in initiating a FLES program are mitigated. Administratively this procedure also has the virtue of involving a minimal commitment. One need face the problems of staffing for only one additional year, whereas the start of a continuous program at the third grade clearly entails assuming these responsibilities for all the subsequent years as well. And certainly this procedure does extend the total time possible for language study.

The chief objection to this procedure is that, in our experience, at least, it vitiates one of the chief reasons for beginning foreign languages early, the opportunity the student thus has to develop an acceptable pronunciation and reasonable fluency.

Our experience has yielded data concerning students starting at various points between the third and sixth grades. Most of our information concerns the relative advantages of starting in the third or the fourth grade. But transfer students furnished some incidental data (though rather meager) concerning beginners at the fifth and sixth grades also.

Our most extensive material was collected in the first two years of our program. In 1955 all students in the third and fourth grades began the study of French and studied the same materials in essentially the same fashion under the same teachers for the next two years.

Roughly seventy-five children were in each grade, and each class had approximately twenty-five students in it. At the outset we had the following information about the relative ability of the two grades, based on tests regularly administered by the school. As we have indicated elsewhere, none of this information is especially helpful if one attempts to predict later achievement in French on the basis of it. Be that as it may, our initial information about the children in the two grades consisted of the following data:

TABLE 1

PER CENT OF THIRD AND FOURTH GRADE STUDENTS FALLING IN EACH
QUARTER OF LOCAL PERCENTILES ON THREE TESTS, 1955

	Revised Stanford-Binet, Form L Grade		Chicago Reading Test Form B3[a] Grade		Iowa Every Pupil Arithmetic Test, Form M[a] Grade	
	III	IV	III	IV	III	IV
Fourth quarter .	18	23	24	24	24	23
Third quarter .	21	27	28	28	26	21
Second quarter	27	29	24	24	24	27
First quarter ..	34	21	24	24	26	29

Thus on the reading test the students in the two grades are generally comparable, and the distribution for the arithmetic test is fairly similar. The situation in regard to the intelligence test is another matter. Since for these two grades combined the correlation between IQ and actual achievement in the first year of French amounts to only .28, this difference should not be overemphasized. Nonetheless, it is worth pointing out that the fourth graders show a considerable advantage in the IQ distribution, with an unusual clustering of the third graders in the bottom quarter of the distribution. The data of the table, in fact, do not reveal the full extent of the skew. On the school's norms, the fifth percentile is a score of 107. Among the third graders there were ten students at this point and below (13 per cent rather than the expected 5 per cent); in the fourth grade only 2 or 3 per cent. Even if one minimizes the role of the IQ in elementary language learning, one knows that it will figure largely in relation to other school subjects. Thus many members of the third-grade class were particularly likely to withdraw from the school because of general academic difficulties long before the completion of the language program.

Still another complication appeared once classes were underway. One of the third-grade classes got off to a very poor start. For this section of twenty-five which had the same teacher and the same materials as the other sections, the first year of French did not involve so much instruction in a foreign language as it did the development of habits of listening and being attentive. The home-room teacher had a difficult time with other subjects as well. This section was, in fact, a rather unusual occurrence in the school. But this section raised, at least, the question of whether all third-graders are "ready" for French. At any rate, the difficulties which this section had are reflected in the total third-grade performance.

Pronunciation at the end of one year was rated as follows:

	Per Cent of Third-Grade Students	Per Cent of Fourth-Grade Students
Excellent	10	12
Good	42	53
Fair	39	32
Poor	9	3

Ratings at the end of the second year, now based on a five-point scale in an effort to make finer distinctions over an increasing range, show a similar distribution:

	Per Cent of Third-Grade Students	Per Cent of Fourth-Grade Students
Excellent	9	14
Very good	35	38
Good	40	37
Inferior	14	11
Poor	2	0

These figures suggest certain generalizations though their validity may be limited to programs of our particular type — i.e., those which seek to impart a maximum mastery of the foreign language. For one thing, the third grade is clearly not too early to start this sort of program. The majority of the third graders speak quite well. On the other hand, it is equally obvious that the fourth grade is not too late. If at some age there is eventual loss in the ability to speak a foreign language because of increasing rigidity in the vocal organs and in the habits involved in speech, the fourth graders are no worse off in these regards than are the third graders (of which the one section just mentioned is an extreme example) as well as the scores which show slightly better performance by the fourth graders suggest that, for our type of course at least, even one year's greater maturity, with its consequences such as better attentiveness, is a distinct asset in learning a language in school. But many of the third graders do well; and since the earlier start makes possible one more year of experience with the language, we feel our experience justifies at least this early a start.

The results for aural comprehension tests during these two years tell much the same story.

TABLE 2
RESULTS ON LOCAL AURAL COMPREHENSION TEST
AT END OF FIRST AND SECOND YEARS OF STUDY

	End of First Year		End of Second Year	
Per Cent of Correct Answers	Per Cent of Third-Grade Starters	Per Cent of Fourth-Grade Starters	Per Cent of Third-Grade Starters	Per Cent of Fourth-Grade Starters
75-100	4	14	25	58
50-74	33	39	70	40
25-49	55	26	5	2
0-24	8	1	0	0

At the end of the first year the contrast between the grades in the per cent of students getting less than half the answers right is particularly striking. More than one-half of the third graders fall into this category whereas only slightly more than a quarter of the fourth graders are down in this group. During the following year, both grades made good progress as measured by this test of first-year materials when it was repeated at the end of the second year. But while more than one-half of the fourth graders can now answer 75 per cent or more of the items correctly, only 25 per cent of the third graders can do this well. In short, though the better pupils in the original third grade are doing quite well and are competing on fairly equal terms with the original fourth-grade group, many of the third graders are beginning to lag behind.

In the second year, two additional tests of aural comprehension over second-year materials were given these pupils. The first (a 20-item multiple-choice test similar to the preceding test) gave the following results:

Per Cent of Correct Answers	Per Cent of Third-Grade Starters	Per Cent of Fourth-Grade Starters
75–100	1	12
50–74	56	55
25–49	35	30
0–24	8	3
Range	2–16	2–18
Mean	10.9	10.3
Median	10	11

On this rather simple test, the original third graders do not come off too badly.

The second test, twenty-five definitions which were to be answered by the single appropriate word, was more difficult.

Per Cent of Correct Answers	Per Cent of Third-Grade Starters	Per Cent of Fourth-Grade Starters
75–100	8	17
50–74	6	8
25–49	28	28
0–24	58	47
Range	0–25	0–25
Mean	6.7	9.4
Median	6	8

The contrasting per cents in the top and bottom quarters as well as the differences in the mean and median reveal the extent to which the performance of the original fourth graders was better, though some third graders continued to do very well. A point worthy of note in all the tests is most obviously apparent in this last test where the actual range of scores in each grade covers the total possible range from "all" to "none." Two years of instruction had produced quite varied levels of achievement.

From this point on in the program, comparisons between the two grades become much more difficult and much less exact because of the movement of pupils and the demands of scheduling as well as because of some other factors we have already seen.

Transfers both into and out of the school had become numerous. Our population is always mobile; but our original third grade suffered unusual attrition during these first two years of our program. As a result, our original group of seventy-seven was reduced to forty-nine. This unusual attrition may be due in part to the large numbers of relatively low IQ's in this class. These students might be beginning to have difficulty in keeping the general pace of the school and were being withdrawn.

Transfer students into the school also had to be provided for, and furnishing appropriate instruction was something of a problem. Though there were quite a few of these children, there were not always enough of them to make a section consisting exclusively of them. Yet it seemed inappropriate to mix them with much younger beginners in the regular program. The flexibility of the daily schedule and the availability of staff also caused further complications for this group.

The great diversity of achievement evident after two years of instruction also posed problems. Some sectioning on the basis of performance seemed desirable, and some distinction in the kind of material studied also seemed indicated.

To handle all these problems in ways feasible within the demands of the practical situation required a considerable reshuffling of students at both grade levels. As a result, a number of variables were introduced, factors which may be more influential than the one under investigation. The comparison could be ended at this point and we could limit our conclusions to the statements supported by those data, as was suggested a few paragraphs above.

But the data from subsequent years, though more confused and somewhat more complicated in presentation, seems to us to shed some additional light on the relative progress of the two grades. Hence we present these facts and figures as briefly as possible.

In the third year of the program, the forty-nine pupils remaining from the original third grade were divided into three sections. The top twenty-three students at that time were placed in a section which moved ahead with the program as planned. A second section was constituted as a review section essentially, devoting much of its time to reworking the materials of the previous two years and doing considerable less work with the new third-year materials. This class consisted of twelve average performers from the original group and was brought up to full class size by the addition of the better performers among those pupils who had in the preceding year transferred into the school and begun French at the fourth grade. The remaining fourteen students, who had made the least progress during the first two years, and the fifteen students transferring into the school at the fifth grade were combined into a third section. This section worked with first-year materials. Our hope was that this arrangement would not only provide elementary instruction for the new students but would also give a useful opportunity for complete review to the least successful of our original third-grade starters. As the data reported in chapter 6 will indicate, this latter hope proved vain.

Since these last two sections did not move ahead with the third-year materials, they drop out of further comparisons which must be based on the one regular section of twenty-three students. There is thus a major discontinuity between the preceding data and those which follow. This one regular section results from the operation of a number of selective factors, not the least among which is past achievement in learning French. Its performance cannot be claimed to the "typical" of the achievement of all our original third graders, for it contains slightly less than half the pupils remaining after the processes of attrition had already reduced the original group of third grade beginners to almost half its original size. But under the circumstances this sort of sectioning was required, and once the various sections began to follow different programs, total comparisons become impossible.

This situation of the group which began French in the fourth grade was much less complicated by the time this third year of the program began. The size of this group had been much less diminished by withdrawals from the school. Also a smaller proportion of the remaining pupils had fallen behind the bulk of their classmates. Thus two regular sections, totaling forty-five students could be organized. The bottom nine pupils were placed in a review section by themselves. (Transfer students into the school at this grade level were sufficiently numerous to constitute a separate section of their own consisting of 25 pupils.)

In the third year and thereafter, consequently, we have for comparisons one regular section of twenty-three pupils from the original third grade and two regular sections of forty-five students from the original fourth grade.

As a basis for further comparisons we can, however, turn back and see how the students who constituted these regular sections in the third year of the program had performed on a 20-item aural comprehension test at the end of the *second* year before these sections were formed.

	Third-Grade Starters	Fourth-Grade Starters
Range	8–15	4–18
Mean	12.3	13
Median	13	14

At both grade levels, naturally these selected students perform better than the unselected groups from which they are drawn. But the slight apparent margin between the two grades is about the same for the selected groups as it is for the unselected. The ranges, even after selection remain rather wide. The somewhat greater selectivity applied to the third-grade group than for the fourth graders appears clearly in the pulling up of the lower end of that range.

After the third year of instruction the results for the regular sections on this same test were as follows:

	Third-Grade Starters	Fourth-Grade Starters
Range	12–19	10–20
Mean	15.4	15.3
Median	16	16

Although the fourth-grade starters continue to exhibit a slightly larger range, the selected groups for each grade compete on equal terms. Much the same evidence is given by a fourteen-item test of reading vocabulary also administered at the end of the third year.

	Third-Grade Starters	Fourth-Grade Starters
Range	2–14	2–15
Mean	8.9	9.1
Median	9	9

Up to this point our data have been based on homemade tests of various sorts. The familiar shortcomings of such instruments coupled with the necessity of making them brief enough to fit into available class periods leave open the question whether the tests may simply not have been inadequate to detect existing differences. At the end of the fourth year of the program we were able to use the Co-

TABLE 3

COMPARISON OF SCALED DERIVED SCORES ON CO-OPERATIVE FRENCH TEST,
ELEMENTARY FORM Q MADE BY THIRD AND FOURTH GRADE
STARTERS AFTER FOUR YEARS OF INSTRUCTION

	Reading		Vocabulary	
	Third-Grade Starters	Fourth-Grade Starters	Third-Grade Starters	Fourth-Grade Starters
Range ..	17–57	9–67	36–66	26–67
Mean ...	35.0	34.8	46.6	44.6
Median ..	33	35	44	44
	Grammar		Total	
	Third-Grade Starters	Fourth-Grade Starters	Third-Grade Starters	Fourth-Grade Starters
Range ..	24–57	24–55	28–56	20–63
Mean ..	35.7	35.5	37	37
Median ..	37	37	36	37

operative French Test, Elementary Form Q. This presumably better instrument confirms that, by this stage of the program at least, the regular sections from both grades were still on equal terms.

For the fifth year of the program, comparisons become even more difficult. The third-grade starters continued much as before. But the fourth-grade starters had by this time reached the end of our seven-year elementary school and entered our high school. During this fifth year they were working on a schedule of 200 minutes per week in French class in contrast to 100 minutes per week for the third-grade starters, who were still on an elementary school schedule. Removals from school and absences at testing periods have still further destroyed whatever comparability yet remained in the data.

One additional set of data does, however, have some interest for terminating this comparison between starters at these two grades. These data involve the ten best students in each grade (*a*) who completed all five years and (*b*) for whom complete test results were available. (This latter point makes the groups finally chosen a sample from the better students rather than a list of the best ten in each grade.) Again, for the sake of having a basis of comparison as well as for its own intrinsic interest, we present the material for the fourth year (when the class periods were still of the same length for both grades) as well as the results for the fifth year.

Table 4 tells a story, many parts of which have become familiar in the course of this chapter. The data for these selected students parallel in nearly every respect the findings we have seen up to this point. The fourth graders average slightly higher in IQ and reading scores and also on the Co-operative test in the fourth year of the program. Another familiar feature of all these comparative data is the gap between the very best third-grade students and their classmates next in line. Thus if we consider the Co-operative scores for the fourth year of the program, the best score is made by a fourth-grade starter, Student 4a. But then in the distribution of the third-grade starters a rather large gap intervenes between student 3c's score of 54 and Student 3d's score of 39. In fact this gap is sufficiently large for all the nine remaining fourth graders' scores to fall within it. This same general phenomenon appears again and again in our various data.

Comparisons between the scores made by both grades in the fifth year are scarcely feasible because of the double amount of classroom instruction which the original fourth graders received. But obviously the third-grade starters made good progress during their fifth year and are better off at the end of their *five-year* FLES program than the

TABLE 4

SCORES OF SELECTED THIRD- AND FOURTH-GRADE STARTERS

Student	IQ	Reading Percentile	Co-op Total Fourth Year	Co-op Total Fifth Year
3a	138	92	57	65
3b	140	97	56	63
3c	121	70	54	68
3d	133	60	39	45
3e	161	94	38	47
3f	109	44	36	58
3g	144	84	36	52
3h	145	43	36	50
3i	138	39	32	42
3j	139	87	30	44
Mean	136.8	71	41.4	53.4
4a	137	58	64	71
4b	136	79	47	63
4c	137	58	44	67
4d	144	52	44	63
4e	166	99	43	72
4f	129	76	42	59
4g	156	54	41	63
4h	148	99	40	70
4i	154	86	40	65
4j	123	77	39	64
Mean	144.0	73	44.4	65.7

fourth graders were at the end of their *four-year* one. It is equally clear from the comparison of the two means for the fourth-grade starters that they too benefited considerably from the additional year's experience, especially from the doubling of exposure to French in formal class instruction.

On the basis of the foregoing evidence and our subjective impressions, we can summarize our beliefs about the relative merits of starting in either the third or fourth grade. In our type of program at least, we believe the fourth-graders make the greater progress for the time invested. Our guess is that the one year of additional maturity and of greater adjustment to school procedures is the primary causative factor. We should like to emphasize that this finding is undoubtedly conditioned to a great degree by the nature of our program. We are not enunciating it as a law for all FLES programs. For us, however, both the data and daily impression indicate the fourth grade is the more efficient starting point.

But having reached that conclusion, we are, nonetheless, not prepared to abandon our practice of starting at the third grade. As the tests show, many of the third graders make extremely good progress, and at the end of five FLES years they are further ahead than they would have been had they had only four years by starting a year later. We believe, therefore, that even in our program, the start at the third grade is justified on the ground of this additional year of contact with the language. The FLES student after five years enters high school with a better background than he would otherwise have. Thus while the staff has few doubts that the fourth-grade starters do better, we continue to recommend to the administration of the school that the French program start at the third grade.

Our data for comparisons between grades other than the third and fourth as starting points are minimal since they are based only on transfer students into the school. The groups are small and their comparability may always be questioned. Change of school in itself may be the symptom of consequence of some factors influencing success, and the very process of transition is probably disturbing. Nevertheless we present such data as we have. They are at least in accord with the general, subjective impressions of teachers working in the program. The data were collected in 1958 when a large number of transfer students entered the school and when a great deal of time in our program was devoted to testing.

Pronunciation is, of course, the most critical area. New students at various grades showed the following patterns in comparison with the regular third-grade starters that year.

TABLE 5

RATING OF THE PRONUNCIATION AT END OF ONE YEAR OF STUDENTS
BEGINNING FRENCH IN VARIOUS GRADES, 1958

	Third Grade		Fourth Grade		Fifth Grade		Sixth Grade	
	No.	Per cent	No.	Per cent	No.	Per cent	No.	Per cent
Excellent ..	6	10	2	13	1	8	2	7
Good	26	45	5	31	3	23	2	7
Fair	19	32	5	31	7	54	8	30
Inferior	7	11	4	25	2	15	11	40
Poor	1	2	...	...	...	...	4	16
Total ...	59	100	16	100	13	100	27	100

The data in Table 5 should certainly not be pressed very hard because of the size and composition of the groups. They do suggest, however, that while some students at every level do well, the percentage of students rated "good" and "excellent" declines rather sharply as we move up through the grades.

These results will probably surprise few readers in view of the common opinion that the earlier the start the better the pronunciation. It might seem, however, that, for our kind of program, greater maturity (which we have stressed in our comparisons between the fourth and third grades) might even more favorably influence results in areas other than pronunciation.

But even when comparison is made on the basis of comprehension, as in Table 6, the fifth and sixth graders show no superiority over the younger group.

In sum, however much diffidence we may feel about the reliability of this meager evidence, we find nothing here to cause us to abandon our preference for the third and fourth grades. To be sure, these beginners at later grades used the materials originally prepared for third and fourth grades. One could argue that other materials geared specifically to the maturity and interest of these higher grades would produce different results. We cannot contest this point. We can only say that the materials used were not

TABLE 6

SCORES ON 23-ITEM AURAL COMPREHENSION TEST MADE AT END OF ONE
YEAR BY STUDENTS BEGINNING FRENCH AT VARIOUS GRADES, 1958

Per Cent of Correct Answers	Third and Fourth Grades		Fifth Grade		Sixth Grade	
	No.	Per cent	No.	Per cent	No.	Per cent
90-100 .	7	9	...	...	...	....
75-89 ..	27	33	3	25	9	36
50-74 ..	42	52	7	58	13	52
20-49 ..	5	6	2	17	3	12
0-19 .	...	...	...	...	...	...
Total	81	100	12	100	25	100

clearly inappropriate and that we doubt whether different materials would have produced very different results.

To summarize, then, for our type of program, we are partial to starting at the third or fourth grade on the grounds that this point (1) affords a considerable amount of time for instruction, (2) takes advantage of the younger child's physiological and psychological facility for learning a foreign language, but (3) catches the children at an age when they are generally more ready for serious academic work, and (4) puts foreign language into the program only when the language processes in the native language are firmly enough engrained that exposure to a foreign one will cause a minimum of disturbance.

Many of our third-grade starters do as well as our fourth-grade starters, but more third graders have difficulty (apparently because of less maturity) than do those who start in Grade IV. For those "ready" for foreign language instruction, however, initiation at the third grade seems desirable to us because of the extra year of contact with the language thus provided.

We should like to propose, however, that these general findings be weighed in terms of individual differences among children. Not *all* third graders, or even fourth graders, are ready for foreign language instruction of the sort attempted by our kind of program. (We suspect this fact is true also for FLES programs of other sorts.) For the child who is immature or who has fairly serious personality or academic problems, initial exposure to the foreign language should probably be deferred until he has, if ever, some chance of success. In spite of the great difficulties in scheduling, advising, and all the rest which this procedure involves, flexibility of this sort is of paramount importance. The unready child will not only have an unhappy experience during the first year or two. His deficiency will tend to increase, he will slow down the rest of the group, he will become an increasing burden to the teacher, and he will be hostile for as many years as he is exposed to the foreign language. To avoid such consequences is worth considerable effort. Wherever the start is made and for whatever reasons, sufficient flexibility must be built into the program to take account of the enormous individual differences in this respect.

6   achievement by grade-level

During the five years of the program we attempted to keep a record of the achievement of our students at various levels of instruction. The following chapter (7) will deal with the final achievement of our third- and fourth-grade beginners at the end of their FLES program. The present chapter covers the achievement of the various classes of third-grade starters in each year of the program.

The data in this and the following chapter are suggestive rather than definitive for reasons which are familiar to those working with FLES programs but are sufficiently important to merit brief recounting. The following factors inevitably make all evaluation of FLES programs less accurate than would be desired.

1. There are as yet no standardized tests of achievement for use at this general level. Homemade tests necessarily lack the improvement gained from tryout, multiple editing, and the rest. More important, comparative figures are unavailable for all such tests built for any single program. But borrowing tests from other sources involves so much change and adaptation, because the amount of material covered by FLES courses tends to be small and particularized to each program, that comparability is largely lost.

2. Setting up stringent testing conditions in the earlier grades is difficult to the point of impossibility. The testing devices for aural comprehension, for example, must be extremely simple, and hence poorer students can easily profit from imitating the reactions of their more capable classmates. Wrong possibilities are likely to be greeted with laughter, groans, and superior smiles on the part of the better students. The correct possibility, on the other hand, produces nods and furious marking of the tests. Repressive measures reduce, but do not eliminate these cues. At the lower grades, moreover, the student's reaction to the testing situation, regardless of his ability, often has a marked influence on the results.

3. Tests of pronunciation and fluency (usually major objectives in FLES programs) must be subjective and hence not very reliable for making comparisons from group to group.

4. Measuring fluency, even in a highly subjective fashion, is extremely difficult.

5. All evaluation takes time, particularly any attempts to test pronunciation and fluency, which require individual testing. When class time is limited to 15-20 minutes per day and when after-school hours are difficult or impossible to arrange, taking the time for testing becomes a problem of first magnitude. For example, a 3-minute test for twenty-five students can, when administration time is included, use up a "week." Since even modest efforts at testing the

various skills can cost two to three weeks of class time in an already brief school year, we have had to temper our desire for neat and adequate data to fit the realities of the situation. The testing of some abilities had to be omitted in some years and had to be rather skimpy in others.

6. The large number of transfer students causes the usual difficulties. Transfers out of the school reduce considerably the size of any group studied over four or five years. Transfers into the school cause some inaccuracy in attempting to measure achievement at particular levels.

7. Numerous variables such as changes in staff, changes in materials, changes in evaluation procedures and changes in approach have affected the program yearly. Thus French 1 in 1959-60 is far from an exact replication of French 1 in 1955–56 and is, we believe, a better course. But comparisons between the two are far from exact.

For all these reasons, then, the following data are far from precise; since elaborate statistical treatment of them would merely introduce an appearance of superficial and spurious exactitude, we present them, consequently, without any effort to measure the statistical significance of the observed differences inasmuch as the factors mentioned play a much larger role than chance. At a rough-and-ready level of treatment, however, the findings seem to us a good reflection of our general experience and, within the limits imposed by the conditions listed above, to be fairly good indexes of the facts in connection with certain topics and problems.

Results for French 1. — Table 7 exemplifies some of the difficulties mentioned earlier. For example, we doubt that there were actually only half as many "excellent" pronunciations in the class of 1959–60 as there were in the third grade of 1955–56. Different judges undoubtedly applied different standards, and as the program progressed and the pupils showed what they were capable of, there may have been some tendency to expect more. Probably the most valid single judgment is that of May, 1958. It was the most elaborate effort and the judge was a member of the College

TABLE 7

RATING OF THIRD-GRADE CLASSES ON PRONUNCIATION
END-OF-YEAR MEASUREMENT IN MAY BY DIFFERENT JUDGES
(Per cent)

	1960	1959	1958	1956
Excellent	7	13	10	15
Good	57	50	45	45
Fair	29	24	32	30
Poor	7	13	13	10

staff of the University of Chicago with no connection with our program.

In spite of the obvious crudity of the measures, certain generalizations do appear possible on the basis of these results. Approximately 10 per cent of the pupils have excellent facility in pronunciation and about the same percentage are "poor," though they are of the same age and have had the same experience. If we combine the groups rated "excellent" and "good" (which in our opinion represents a higher level of performance than is usually achieved by more mature beginners), we see that annually 55–65 per cent of our third-grade pupils have attained this very satisfactory level of proficiency.

In Table 8 the standard applied is the same (in contrast to the varying standards of the individual judges in the case of pronunciation), again we see considerable variation, probably due to other variables in the course. Nonetheless, certain fairly sound generalizations can be made.

TABLE 8

AURAL COMPREHENSION SCORES
BASED ON 23-ITEM MULTIPLE CHOICE TEST
(Per cent)

Scores	1960	1958	1956
20–23	17	11	10
15–19	61	50	59
12–14	17	30	23
0–12	5	9	8
Range of scores ...	5–22	8–22	7–23

About 60–80 per cent of the pupils understand two-thirds or more of the material presented, and up to 90 per cent understand at least one-half. At the same time it is equally clear that 5–10 per cent of the children comprehend less than half of the material, with some of them able to deal with only a third or a quarter. With this low level of achievement on a very limited amount of material which has been presented slowly during this first year, there is little hope that this group will find further work with the language a happy and productive experience, particularly in view of the fact that some of their classmates have mastered the total amount of material almost perfectly.

In addition to the two preceding measures which were used with some regularity, we tried various other measures of oral skill. In the spring of 1960 we undertook the evaluation of fluency in our third graders in two different ways. The first was on the basis of the completeness and accuracy of their response to ten oral questions. The distribution of achievement as averaged over the ten questions was as follows:

Rating	Number of Students	Per Cent of Students
Excellent	9	17
Good	27	52
Fair	12	23
Poor	4	8
	52	100

The second sort of evaluation was based on the completeness and correctness of their description of nine pictures. For a rating of "excellent," a description of all nine pictures was required; students rated "poor" could offer a description of two or fewer pictures. The distribution of ratings was as follows:

Rating	Number of Students	Per Cent of Students
Excellent	15	29
Good	19	36
Fair	13	25
Poor	5	10
	52	100

All these measures of various third-grade classes tell roughly the same story. From 10 to 15 per cent of the students are doing excellent work by anyone's standards. Two-thirds of the group are quite clearly benefiting from an early introduction to French and taking advantage of the opportunity. The achievement of the other third is less impressive. To be sure, this fact is true of the lower third in almost any distribution of academic performance. We have always been concerned, however, with that 5–10 per cent who are clearly less than competent (as chapter 4 indicated.) Moreover, it is not a matter merely of being that tail which any distribution must have. These students are scarcely competing on the same scale. Thus, to take as our example the test mentioned last, it is not a matter of their descriptions of the nine pictures being in French sentences which are less complete and correct than their classmates who rated "excellent" or "good." The students rated "poor" could not make even incomplete or incorrect attempts for more than one or two pictures. Clearly these students were going to constitute a problem in subsequent years.

It can, of course, be argued (as we ourselves have considered) that this performance is simply a product of the amount of material we had assigned to this year and of the level of mastery required. Having seen that 10 per cent of our pupils were in real trouble and that about a third of them were performing at a level we could describe as no better than "fair," should we not have reduced the load, slowed the pace, and taken a number of other actions designed to make it possible for nearly all members of the group to be rated "good." After giving these possibilities serious thought, we did not make any of these drastic alterations in our program for several reasons.

First, we felt that reducing the material and slowing the pace, though a plausible remedy, would actually be ineffectual. As we indicated in chapter 4, their essential difficulties (difficulties in adjusting to school, family problems,

100

personality problems) were not amenable to treatment by altering the program.

Second, even had such a decision seemed wholly justifiable, it was not fully in our power to make. Some FLES programs have apparently felt freer to give the children such experience with the foreign language as nearly all of them can take without difficulty. But our experiment hinged on the possibility that the five years of French in elementary school would produce linguistic competence equivalent to three or four semesters' work in high school. Though the pace would inevitably quicken, too relaxed an approach in the first year would constitute a handicap which even the ablest students could never overcome in later years.

Results for French 2. — Analysis of the work of French 2 (fourth grade) indicated no marked change in the level of pronunciation from that attained at the end of the French 1. Comprehension and fluency in regard to the new materials remained proportionately the same for individual students. But gradually the poorer students were beginning to suffer more and more from the cumulation of deficiencies which began in French 1. Testing at the end of the year revealed a wide range in achievement at this point in the program.

Pronunciation (now measured on a five-point scale rather than the four-point one because of the widening range) was rated as follows:

Rating	Per Cent of Students 1958	Per Cent of Students 1960
Excellent	11	11
Very good	36	35
Good	39	35
Inferior	12	11
Poor	2	8

Once again, despite probable variation in the judges' standards, the distributions for the two years for whom this rating was made are fairly similar.

Aural comprehension at this stage was only once tested

101

with an instrument sufficiently long to make the results reliable, a 40-item test used as a final examination in May, 1960. The following distribution was obtained:

Per Cent of Material	Number of Students	Per Cent of Students
90–100	5	11
75–89	12	27
50–74	20	44
0–49	8	18

In short, while 11 per cent of the students were able to answer almost all forty items correctly, 18 per cent of them were unable to cope with even half of them.

The seriousness of the gap occurring between levels of achievement within the same class or even the same section is nowhere so apparent as in the matter of fluency. The problem can be illustrated by the rating of a typical section of twenty-one pupils in 1960, with the scores recorded as percentages of the total points possible on a rating scale for each utterance:

Per Cent of Possible Points	Number of Students	Per Cent of Students
90–100	4	19
70–89	6	29
50–69	4	19
0–49	7	33

The problems caused by this gap between those making fair progress and those making little progress had at this level of instruction become so pressing that various attempts to deal with it directly are indicated for French 3.

Results for French 3. — The third year of our program involves various complexities in teaching and scheduling. Some of these are brought about by those differences in the learning rate we have just seen. Other complications arise from transfer students into the school.

In an effort to take care of both these problems in 1957–58, the first year our program reached this third year, classes were organized at three different levels. The twenty-three better pupils in French 3A went on to new materials as

102

originally planned. The twelve mediocre students in French 3B (grouped with the better students who had entered the school and began French the preceding year) spent the year primarily in reviewing the materials of the first two years. In French 3C, the fourteen poorest students from French 2 and twelve transfer students into the school (who had had no previous experience with French) were given what was essentially French 1.

The group in French 3A (or what was really the third year of French), relieved of the drag of the poorer students, had a very successful year, continuing with oral-aural work and systematically gaining a wider experience with reading.

The relative ineffectiveness of the review for students in French 3B and 3C can be seen by examining various scores shown in Table 9 on the comprehension test usually given at the end of French 1. In this group which reviewed the materials of the first two years, some improvements on this French 1 test are observable. Thus 29 per cent of the students (as compared with the 10 per cent at the end of French 2) have mastered at least three-fourths of the ma-

TABLE 9

SCORES ON REPETITION OF FRENCH 1 TEST BY STUDENTS OF FRENCH 3B COMPARED WITH THEIR STANDING IN SAME TEST AT END OF FRENCH 2

Per Cent of Material Correct	Per Cent of Students Tested in French 2	Per Cent of Students Tested in French 3B
90–100	0	5
75–89	10	24
50–74	76	57
20–49	14	14
0–19	0	0

terials of French 1. But in view of the amount of review to which this group was subjected, one would have hoped that 75–90 per cent of the students (rather than 29 per cent) would have achieved this much mastery of the first-year materials. Even more dismaying is the fact that by the end of this, their third year of French, 14 per cent of the group were no better off than they were at the end of French 2 and still have not mastered even one-half of the material presented in the first year. Repetition and review are obviously not an adequate answer to the problem of "saving" those students who had begun to drop behind by the end of French 2. Probably the reasons for the failure of this procedure are those mentioned earlier in chapter 4.

Even more disconcerting was the performance of the students in French 3C, who were essentially given a repetition of French 1 because of their poor showing in French 1 and French 2. Their failure to progress — in fact, their tendency to regress — is startling, both when compared with their own scores at the end of French 2 and when compared with their classmates who were transfer students, working through the first-year materials for the first time. The scores shown in Table 10 are based on the twelve of the fourteen third-grade starters remaining in 3C at the end of the third year.

TABLE 10

Scores on French 1 Test, of Students in French 3C (1958) Compared with Their Scores at End of French 2 (1957) and with Those of Transfer Students Starting French

Per Cent of Materi- al Correct	Number of "old" French 3C Students Tested at End of French 2	Number of "old" French 3C Students Tested at End of French 3C	Number of Transfer Students in French 3C
90–100	0	0	0
75–89	0	1	3
50–74	11	5	7
20–49	1	6	2

Specifically, only one of the "old" students managed to improve to the point of mastering at least three-quarters of the first-year materials. Five of them actually managed to do worse than they had at the end of the previous year. Quite clearly something other than lack of adequate con-

104

tact with the materials to be learned is responsible for their lack of achievement, even if we make all possible allowance for the limitations on interesting and effective review of narrow first-year materials. If we pass over the one student who achieved 75 per cent mastery, there were eleven of our original third-grade starters who had spent two years on the first-year materials and had also been exposed to the second-year work; but they still had no mastery of the most elementary materials. One is even inclined to wonder how much damage they managed to do to the transfer students in their section since these latter did somewhat below the likely expectation for performance in French 1.

Grouping on the basis of ability obviously benefited these poorer students very little. And it is equally obvious that the repetition and review is far from a panacea for students falling behind in French 1 and 2. A particularly sobering note was sounded by the further fact that those students would have to be "carried" for two more years in some fashion or other within our program.

French 4. — As the preceding section indicated, by the third year the problems of sectioning students becomes complicated. In the fourth year the difficulty is further exacerbated. The range of achievement among the "old" students continually widens. Transfer students into the four grades must be appropriately provided for in ways which will fit the rest of their schedules. As a result of these and other factors there is always a considerable shuffling of students at this level, and the different sections have had rather different programs. As a result, though we have comparative data for this year too, the figures seem to us essentially meaningless because of the variation in all factors. Consequently we present instead the following figure which indicates the general flow of students in our program. Then we shall pass immediately to the fifth and final year of our program. Achievement can be more easily measured meaningfully at that point.

The general movement shown in the chart can be sum-

FIGURE 1

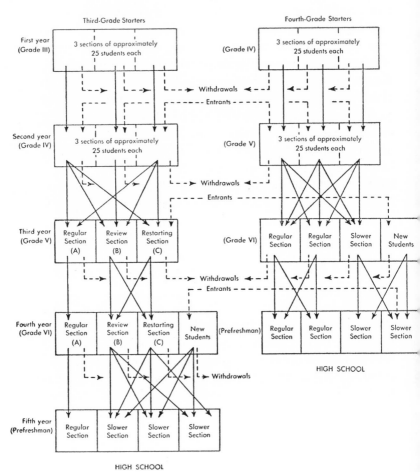

marized fairly simply though, as the arrows indicate, the details are complex. The chief reason for the complication is the continual flow of students in and out of the school and hence in and out of our program. Appropriate instruction with classmates of approximately their own age and grade had to be provided for the newcomers. At the same time the size of the language classes could not be allowed to deviate much from that of other classes in the school. Consequently the gaps caused by withdrawals had to be

106

filled as much as possible by later entrants into the program. Meeting all these requirements involved considerable shuffling of the students.

In the first two years the situation was relatively simple. There were three undifferentiated classes in each grade. The dropouts at the end of the first year were replaced by students new to the school who were given special tutoring to enable them to catch up.

With the start of the third year, the situation became more complicated, and we now follow the course of the third-grade starters, ignoring the fourth-grade starters for the moment. For the third-grade starters, three sections were organized. Section A continued on schedule and is the class most typical of our FLES program and one which we shall report on at greater length in the next chapter. We attempted to keep its personnel unchanged in the last three years of the program. Section B consisted of students doing less well in the first two years of work, and they formed the basis of a slower section for the following years. Section C was composed of the poorest students in the original group. They were combined with new entrants at their same grade to form a section which began again from the start.

In the fourth year the organization of the third-grade starters remained much the same as in the preceding year. Section A continued essentially unchanged as the class on schedule. Section B moved at a slightly slower pace, and Section C at a still slower pace. There was some interchange of pupils between Sections B and C on the basis of achievement. During this fourth year, the number of entrants was sufficiently large for them to constitute a class of their own. The fifth and last year followed much the same pattern. Section A remained the section on schedule, and the other three sections moved at various slower paces, with the pupils apportioned among them on the basis of achievement. The few students entering the school in this last elementary year (Prefreshman) were not taken into the FLES program.

The pattern for the group beginning in the fourth grade was rather similar. In the third year of their program, two sections continued on schedule, and one moved at a slower pace. Entrants made up a special class. In the fourth and last year of this program, the two regular sections were kept essentially unchanged, but there was some interchange of students between the two slower sections.

Because of this continual shift in student personnel of many of the sections, data are, for the most part, not comparable, except for the regular sections. Consequently we shall move in the next two chapters to the results available from these groups.

notes to chapter 6

Evaluation, particularly objective measurement, is a matter of prime concern to all workers in FLES. Though anecdotal reports of successful programs may seem quite sufficient to advocates of FLES, such testimony does not always carry equal conviction in decision-making circles: school boards, school administrators, and grade-school faculties at large. In these circumstances it is particularly unfortunate that the areas of oral skill, where FLES students are likely to be especially strong, are precisely those in which objective measurement is difficult, if not impossible, to achieve.

Progress and possibilities in this area are reported by Nelson Brooks in "Language Competences and Testing" in *Report of the Northeast Conference on the Teaching of Foreign Languages* (New York: New York University Press, 1957), pp. 21–23 and *ibid.*, (1959), pp. 50–59.

In the meantime, efforts at evaluation have taken varied forms, and rather different judgments have been reached. The following articles indicate the variety in both respects: "A Symposium on Foreign Languages in the Elementary School," *NEA Journal*, XLIX (Feb., 1960), 33–36; Joseph Justman and Martin L. Nass, "The High School Achievement of Pupils Who Were and Were Not Introduced to a Foreign Language in Elementary School," *Modern Language Journal*, XL (Mar., 1956), 120–23; Emile B. De Sauzé, "Continuity and Articulation in the Study of Foreign Languages between Elementary and Senior High School," *French Review*, XXVIII (May, 1955), 536–37; Elizabeth Etnire, "Five Years of Spanish in the Elementary School," *Modern Language Journal*, XLII (Nov., 1958), 349–51; B. W. Haseltine, "French for Elementary Schools," *Modern Language Journal*, XLIII (Jan., 1960), 43; Blanche Price, "Memories of French in Elementary School," *French Review*, XXIX (Jan., 1956), 245–49; Edith Kern, "FLES Testing," *French Review*, XXXIII (Oct., 1959), 45–52; with the reply of Robert Brooks in a "Letter to the Editor," *ibid.*, (Apr., 1960), 506–8.

7 terminal achievement

If the proof of the pudding is in the eating, clearly the vital question is what level of achievement our pupils ultimately attained. And since our program aimed at the mastery of the linguistic skills to the extent that FLES experience would afford advanced standing in high school, our primary problem was to measure these competencies by tests typical of the sort customarily used.

As we have pointed out, the usual testing devices for placement and credit are inappropriate and even unfair to FLES students. Standardized tests are not available for measuring fluency and correctness of speaking, an area where FLES students excel. On the other hand, available examinations tend to be weighted heavily with questions on formal grammar (sometimes relatively abstruse points) in which FLES students have little training. Nonetheless, if FLES programs like ours are to be part of the usual educational scene, unfair though it may be they must be able to meet this kind of challenge. Programs with other objectives in other situations, where the linguistic skills receive less emphasis, may not need to face this issue so directly. But courses like ours will stand or fall by the degree of language mastery demonstrated, even though important areas of oral competence are slighted or ignored by the tests. Hence, from the start we have sought to use the measures commonly accepted by academic institutions.

In this chapter we shall focus on those students who began French in the third grade in 1955 and who completed our program in June, 1960. These students had taken the full five years of our FLES program for a total of approximately 260 contact hours.

This total of 260 hours merits at least passing comment. It is the number of scheduled class hours, but far from all this time was devoted to instruction. For example, even our modest testing program reduced considerably the time for teaching. Participation in school events such as Christmas programs also takes time from the scheduled work. In the lower grades, where class periods are short, the necessary details of classroom management (getting the class arranged and attentive, distributing materials, etc.) consume a formidable proportion of the 15 or 20 minutes. Matters like these account for great loss in class time, even without raising the question of whether the teacher uses the remaining time efficiently. The 260 class hours represent, therefore, considerably less than 260 hours of instruction.

Not all 75 students who began the program in Grade III completed it or completed it on schedule. This situation can be summarized as follows:

Completed program on schedule 20
Down-graded to slower sections 25
Withdrawn from school 30
                                                                    ——
                                                                    75

Thus, 58 per cent of our original starters completed the five years of the program with us, and only 27 per cent of the original beginners completed it on schedule as planned. As was to be expected in as mobile a community as ours, 40 per cent of those who started the program left it because they left the school, whether permanently or temporarily. This was a form of attrition over which we had no control, and it affected students at all levels of achievement. A few transfer students into the school with backgrounds in French were added to the sections of this group over the years, but their records are not included here.

As was indicated in the preceding chapter, some further attrition occurred within the last three years of the program as students were unable to keep pace and were transferred to slower sections. Thus, in the third year, the remaining 45 children were divided between two sections, 20 in Section A, a more advanced section, and 25 in Section B, a slower section. Though conversation was still stressed, in both sections a standard grammar was used. Section A, however, used a second-year high-school text; Section B, a first-year.

Section A represents, therefore, those who truly completed the program. Section B contained the students less successful with the five years' work. As the results indicate in Table 11, some of the children in Section B managed to learn astonishingly little.

We offer both sets of norms because neither of them is wholly appropriate. The level of performance in the private schools supplying norms is considerably above that of the public schools. One factor probably operating here is that the private schools can select its student body. As a private school which feeds students into our own high school, we

TABLE 11

PERFORMANCE IN SCALED SCORES OF FIFTH-YEAR FLES STUDENTS,
SECTIONS A AND B, ON CO-OPERATIVE FRENCH TEST, ELEMENTARY
FORM Q, COMPARED WITH NORMS FOR INDEPENDENT AND
PUBLIC SECONDARY SCHOOLS

	Reading	Vocabulary	Grammar	Total
Section A:				
Range	23–67	37–72	24–62	26–68
Mean	42.1	53.5	45.2	45.7
Mean	41	55	45	44
Section B:				
Range	2–39	22–45	4–44	14–40
Mean	17.0	33.2	33.2	24.9
Median	17	30	34	24
	Means for Independent Secondary Schools			
1 Semester	34.1	37.2	38.9	35.4
2 Semesters	45.3	54.6	52.2	50.7
3 Semesters	53.2	59.4	57.6	57.4
4 Semesters	60.1	63.8	63.1	63.7
	Means for Public Secondary Schools			
1 Semester	26.3	31.2	32.0	27.5
2 Semesters	41.8	47.2	47.5	45.0
3 Semesters	50.3	54.2	53.4	53.0
4 Semesters	57.6	60.1	58.8	59.8

probably should use the private-school norms in regard to
advanced standing and general articulation with high-
school work. But in regard to achievement, the norms are
perhaps unfairly high. A selective *elementary* school is considerably different from a selective *secondary* school simply
because the bases and means of selection in the kindergarten or Grade I are quite different from those possible
and usually employed in Grade IX.

In either case, moreover, secondary-school norms are
possibly unduly high for several other reasons. The secondary-school pupil often has a choice among languages or
even whether to take a modern language at all. All our third
graders in 1955 were required to take French. In the secondary school, students who do not do well may drop, or
be dropped from, the course before the end of the semester

or the end of the year when their scores would enter the norms. Our students were "locked" into our program for the full five years if they remained in the school. Students doing poorly not only lowered final averages, they had a similar effect in the pace and tone of some sections throughout several years of our program. Finally, our "five years" involved about 260 class hours as compared with 265 class hours for "two years" in our own high school, with most high schools having a still longer school year. These high-school years are always supplemented by a certain amount of homework. In our FLES program out-of-class contact with language is negligible. In sum, any norms based on secondary-school work are fundamentally an improper basis for comparison.

Leaving the norms out of account for the moment and looking only at the relative performance of our two sections on this test, one must be struck by the enormous differences between the means and especially the medians. This latter phenomenon is, of course, partly the function of an equally striking fact, the differences in the ranges of scores made by the two sections, especially the lower limit of the range for Section B. While some of the children of Section B fall within the range of Section A, the lower limit of B's range falls far below that of A's, with some of the children in Section B having learned very little within the scope of this test. The tremendous range of scaled scores if both sections are combined (in reading, for example, 2–67, with five of the pupils in Section B scoring only 2) again documents the great differences in capacity and development even among children in a selected school population. Even within Section A alone, the range is large, with some pupils turning in a very impressive performance while others were doing much less well.

If we compare the mean scores, we see that section A falls slightly short of the mean for one year's work in the independent secondary schools furnishing the norms for this test. The achievement of Section B is considerably less satisfactory, falling considerably farther short of the mean for even one semester. For both groups, the sub-score on vocabulary tends to be the best, a result to be expected when this sort of test is used on students trained predominantly by the oral-aural method since this part fits their kind of training best.

The achievement of the entire group (Sections A and B combined) can probably best be seen in Table 12 where all 45 students are distributed over the grid formed by the norms for independent secondary schools for one to four semesters of work. Almost 50 per cent of the total group achieved the equivalent of the median student completing one semester's work in an independent secondary school. Of the group 11 per cent does as well as the average or better student after two semesters, and almost as many meet this norm for three semesters' work. Even gross inspection of these figures suggests that while the performance of many of our students on this test is not impressive, about 10 per cent of them are doing astonishingly well.

TABLE 12

Number of Students in French 5 Falling in the Various Quarters of the Norms for Independent Secondary Schools for One, Two, Three and Four Semesters

	1 Semester	2 Semesters	3 Semesters	4 Semesters
Fourth quarter ...	13	4	2	0
Third quarter ...	9	1	2	2
Second quarter ..	3	6	1	2
First quarter	20	34	40	41

The results of the Co-operative French Listening Comprehensive Test shown in Table 13 are a more valid examination since they measure an ability in which our students have been trained.

If we distribute the combined sections over the quartiles of the norms for two and three years work in high school, we get the picture shown in Table 14.

TABLE 13

SCALED SCORES OF SECTIONS A AND B ON CO-OPERATIVE FRENCH LISTENING
COMPREHENSION TEST COMPARED WITH NORMS FOR TWO AND
THREE YEARS OF HIGH-SCHOOL STUDY

	Section A	Section B	Norm for 2 years	Norm for 3 years
Range	178–210	160–184	...	...
Median	194	170.5	...	...
Mean	190.5	168.7	188.2	197.1

TABLE 14

NUMBER OF STUDENTS IN SECTIONS A AND B COMBINED FALLING IN EACH
QUARTER OF THE NORMS FOR TWO AND THREE YEARS OF
STUDY IN HIGH SCHOOL*

	Two Years of High School	Three Years of High School
Fourth quarter	3	1
Third quarter	8	3
Second quarter	8	8
First quarter	22	29

* Two students were absent from each section on the day this test was
administered; hence, N equals 41 for this test.

With one important exception, these two tables indicate
much the same situation as that depicted by the preceding
test. The exception is the fact that here the scores of Section A (those completing our program) compare quite
favorably with those of students who have completed two
years of high-school work. Since this was the general level
of achievement we hoped our pupils could attain, these
results are very gratifying. Otherwise, the notable features
of the findings are similar to those of the preceding test.
The scores cover a wide range. Four students of Section A
turn in extremely good performances, exceeding the mean
for three years of work in high school. About the same number of students from Section B are equally far at the other
extreme; they have acquired in five years as little skill in
aural comprehension as they have in those areas measured
by the preceding test.

116

A final rating on pronunciation is of some interest. For the nineteen students of Group A tested, the evaluation was as follows:

Rating	No. of Students	Per Cent of Students
Excellent	7	37
Good	11	58
Fair	1	5
Poor	0	0
	19	100

In short, with one exception all students completing the program on schedule were "good" or better with respect to pronunciation. As can be seen from comparing the ratings given all students at the end of the first year (Excellent 15 per cent, Good 45 per cent, Fair 30 per cent, and Poor 10 per cent), general attrition and the selection through sectioning have probably removed most of those weak in pronunciation. It seems doubtful that basic pronunciation changed markedly over the years though improvement was always sought.

The tables on the preceding pages give our best description of our group as a whole, or at least the two sections into which it was ultimately divided. But these figures tend to be misleading in several different fashions. They appear more exact than they in fact are, and they tend to conceal some points about students' progress through our program which seem to us of major importance. Consequently we feel it useful to present a longitudinal study in Table 15 of fifteen students, portraying their fate in the course of the full program.

The students were selected in the following fashion. Five of them (Students A-E) were clearly "good" students on the basis of their first year's work; five of them (Students K-0) were "average" students; and five of them (V-Z) were definitely "poor." Those selected were not necessarily the five highest or lowest or closest to the median. They were chosen primarily as illustrative of certain facts about stu-

TABLE 15
Longitudinal Study of Fifteen Students During Full FLES Program

Student	IQ (1)	Age (2)	Chicago Reading Test-B3a (1956)		Iowa Every Pupil Arithmetic Test Form Ma		Aural Comprehension 45 Items (7)	Pronunciation 4 = Excellent (8)
			Grade (3)	Local Percentile (4)	Grade (5)	Local Percentile (6)		
A	121	8.5	4.0	70	6.6	99	42	4
B	138	8.5	6.0	92	4.7	54	37	4
C	144	8.8	5.4	84	5.5	92	37	3
D	140	8.8	6.8	97	5.4	89	37	3
E	161	8.2	6.6	94	5.6	94	34	3
K	134	8.5	3.2	35	5.5	92	31	2
L	130	7.11	5.8	89	4.3	35	29	4
M	104	8.4	4.4	70	4.1	22	30	3
N	161	7.10	2.8	24	5.1	79	29	2
O	126	8.6	5.8	89	4.6	49	27	3
V	156	7.11	2.4	9	3.8	18	23	1
W	169	8.9	3.4	39	5.5	92	20	1
X	105	8.11	2.8	27	3.7	14	14	3
Y	97	8.6	4.0	60	3.6	8	18	2
Z	125	7.11	4.0	60	4.3	35	5	2

Preliminary Data: columns 1–6. First Year: columns 7–8.

TABLE 15 (cont.)

LONGITUDINAL STUDY OF FIFTEEN STUDENTS
DURING FULL FLES PROGRAM

Student	Second Year					Third Year		
	Pronunciation 4 = Excellent (9)	Aural Comprehension 23 Items (10)	Completion 25 Items (11)	Aural Comprehension 20 Items (12)	Total Aural 68 Items (13)	Section (14)	Reading-Vocabulary 14 Items (15)	Aural Comprehension 20 Items (16)
A	4	23	25	15	63	A	14	..
B	4	21	20	15	56	A	12	19
C	3	22	17	14	53	A	12	14
D	3	19	21	15	55	A	11	18
E	4	21	19	14	54	A	5	..
K	2	17	10	11	38	B	4	16
L	4	16	8	9	33	A	8	15
M	3	17	7	14	38	A	11	14
N	2	17	1	8	26	B	7	5
O	3	18	9	11	38	A	..	16
V	2	15	10	10	35	B	5	8
W	1	16	4	7	27	C	..	..
X	3	14	0	9	23	C	0	3
Y	3	11	2	..	..	B	3	7
Z	2	16	3	12	31	C	0	..

TABLE 15 (cont.)

LONGITUDINAL STUDY OF FIFTEEN STUDENTS DURING FULL FLES PROGRAM

Student	Fourth Year — Co-operative Test Form Q Percentiles For Two Semesters at a Private School				Section (21)	Fifth Year — Co-operative Test Form Q Percentiles For Two Semesters at a Private School			
	Reading (17)	Vocabulary (18)	Grammar (19)	Total (20)		Reading (22)	Vocabulary (23)	Grammar (24)	Total (25)
A	74	89	19	63	A	97	97	85	96
B	53	89	62	74	A	85	91	82	92
C	10	9	5	6	A	60	60	54	55
D	86	43	70	71	A	90	91	85	90
E	42	35	1	10	A	42	60	14	35
K	1	1	1	1	B	1	1	14	1
L	7	21	1	4	A	35	24	29	10
M	:	1	5	:	A	45	64	5	28
N	1	:	1	1	B	22	2	25	10
O	:	:	:	:	A	10	6	17	6
V	1	1	1	1	C	1	4	1	1
W	1	1	1	1	C	1	1	1	1
X	1	1	1	1	C	1	3	1	1
Y	1	1	1	1	B	5	1	1	1
Z	1	1	1	1	C	1	1	1	1

TABLE 15 (cont.)

LONGITUDINAL STUDY OF FIFTEEN STUDENTS
DURING FULL FLES PROGRAM

Fifth Year

Student	Co-operative Test Form Q Percentiles for Four Semesters at a Private School				Co-operative Aural Comprehension (30)	Pronunciation 4 = Excellent (31)
	Reading (26)	Vocabulary (27)	Grammar (28)	Total (29)		
A	74	81	45	67	87	4
B	43	63	41	55	90	4
C	12	24	14	11	74	4
D	46	63	45	47	92	3
E	5	24	1	4	71	4
K	1	1	1	1	7	3
L	3	4	4	1	50	3
M	6	27	2	1	44	3
N	1	1	3	1	17	3
O	1	1	2	1	38	3
V	1	1	1	1	21	3
W	1	1	1	1	:	1
X	1	1	1	1	2	2
Y	1	1	1	1	2	2
Z	1	1	1	1	1	3

dent performance at these levels, and all of them must have completed the full five years in order to be chosen. A further factor in selection was an effort to get students for whom complete data were available. But absence is a common phenomenon in the elementary school, and in our situation the administration of "make-up" exams is generally impossible. Hence, even with selection, our typical students present quite a few blanks in the table of data.

Students A and B are among the very top of the class at the start and continued to perform at that same level for the next four years. In terms of the tests, their five "years" of FLES have quite clearly been worth two years of high-school work, and the accuracy and fluency of their speech probably exceeds that of the high-school student. This is the kind of experience which, in our opinion, clearly justifies our FLES program. If all students had this type of experience, there would be little argument about the value of FLES. Unfortunately students A and B represent only the upper third (or even part of it) of our students. In passing, one can note that nothing about the preliminary data suggests that these students are outstanding as compared to others in the list who fare quite differently.

Students C and E appear weaker, but this impression is partly the creation of our tests. In the Co-operative Tests in both the fourth and fifth years (cols. 17–29), they make poor showings. But the fact that these tests are inappropriate to the course must be kept in mind. Their pronunciation (cols. 8, 9, 31) moves from "good" to "excellent" and their aural comprehension is always at a high level (cols. 7, 13, 30).

The development of the "median" students is more complex, as is exemplified by the five reported here. By the end of the second year, they are, by and large, performing quite obviously at a level below the upper third of the group (cols. 7–13) though they are not doing badly. These scores and their behavior in the classroom were taken into account when these average students were sectioned for the third year of work (col. 14). The better of these average students, like L, M, and O in our chart, were placed in Section A with the better students. The hope was that such students could probably keep up with the normal pace, and that, if so, they could have the eventual benefit of the full FLES program as planned. By and large this hope was justified. In the third year (cols. 15, 16) they perform at a level quite appropriate to their status in Section A. In the fourth and fifth years their scores on the Co-operative Test are poor, not merely in comparison with the norms but also in comparison with the performance of our better students such as A-E. This point exemplifies a striking fact which appears in all our data based on tests (homemade or standardized) intended for older students. While our better FLES students compete on fairly equal terms with the better high-school students, our average FLES students do much less well than the medium high-school students (and our poorest FLES students do even more abominably than their high-school counterparts). But, as in the case of the better students, if we do not give undue weight to these tests and look at more appropriate measures (cols. 30, 31), we see that "average" students of this sort give "good, average" performances.

Other students in this middle group were like students K and N, who on the basis of formal and informal evidence seemed unlikely to be able to keep up. They were, consequently, placed in Section B (col. 14) at the beginning of the third year. This section as was indicated earlier (supra p. 85) was essentially a review section. Both K and N did fairly well in aural comprehension (cols. 7, 13) but both had trouble with oral work (cols. 8, 9). In the fourth and fifth years both did very poorly on the two administrations of the Co-operative Test, but unlike the preceding cases we have examined, they also did poorly in aural comprehension (col. 30), and K's pronunciation remained only fair. This tendency of some of our "medium" students to fall toward the lower levels of achievement is, of course, related to the other trend we noted earlier — the tendency for our average elementary school students to do less well than average high-school students.

The poorer students (V-Z), though not conspicuous in terms of the preliminary data, are revealed with considerable clarity by their aural and oral scores for the first year (cols. 7 and 8). At the end of the second year, the aural comprehension scores of students V and Z are perhaps suspiciously high. Since the testing situation is very simple, imitation of their more able classmates may account for these students' relative success here. We must acknowledge, however, that Student V did ultimately achieve a percentile score of 21 on a standardized test (col. 30). At any rate, students like V and Y were placed in the review section, B, while W, X, Z, and eight others like them were placed with transfer students in Section C, which was first year French. Though absences make our records incomplete, Students W, X, and Z performed about as expected. In the following year, the sections were constituted much as before (col. 21) though in this year the poorer students were again combined with new beginners at the 6th grade level. Aside from the aural-comprehension score of Student V, all of them do very poorly in the fourth and fifth year tests. The tremendous gap separating these poorer students from the "better" students who began French with them five years before is well reflected in the percentile scores of columns 25 and 30. Clearly, students like these gained little, if any, language mastery from the program. As we shall see in chapter 8, the experience was not, however, traumatic, and they may well have gained some insight into language and into French culture, objectives not measured by our present tests.

These records also exemplify another major point: the relative consistency of student performance over the years. If, for example, we compare the rank order of achievement in aural comprehension at the end of the first year (col.

7) with that at the end of five years (col. 30), we find few surprises. Student C has slipped somewhat: on the basis of his first year's performance we might expect his percentile score in column 30 to be closer to 90 than 74. (His other Co-operative Test score is also surprisingly low.) But even his actual score keeps him well with the group of top achievers. Students K and N also seem to have slumped in column 30, but these scores are largely an artifact of the sectioning recorded in column 14. Their inclusion in Section B, with its emphasis on review during the third year automatically limited their exposure to new material and made it highly probable that they would receive relatively much lower scores on later standardized tests than those like L, M and O, who carried on regular work in Section A. The performance of the "poorer" students (like V-Z) is distressingly true to form, with Student V's 21 in column 30 being truly surprising.

Nonetheless, the geese do not turn into swans. Thus, in the case of a student like Z (and we have a number like him), we can foresee fairly well what the situation will be four years later in columns 25, 29, 30, and 31. Hence, we shall continue to attempt to find ways appropriate to our situation of so handling such cases that they gain as much as possible from their FLES experience, even if they learn little or no French.

Fundamentally the program was planned for those students who began French in Grade III. But at the same time we also had students starting in Grade IV. Though this group would have only four rather than five years of FLES instruction, we naturally sought to make their experience as worthwhile as possible.

At the end of their fourth and last FLES year, their scores on the Co-operative Test shown in Table 16 stood as follows when compared with the norms.

As a glance at the table shows, this group did somewhat better than the one-semester average for both public and private schools but falls far short of the average for one

TABLE 16

SCALED SCORES ON CO-OPERATIVE FRENCH TEST, FORM Q, MADE BY
FOURTH-GRADE STARTERS AFTER FOUR YEARS OF INSTRUCTION AS
COMPARED WITH MEANS FROM NORMS FOR PRIVATE
AND SECONDARY SCHOOLS

	Reading	Vocabulary	Grammar	Total
Range	9–67	26–67	24–55	20–63
Mean	34.8	44.6	35.5	37
Median	35	44	37.	37
	Means for Independent Secondary Schools			
1 Semester	34.1	37.2	38.9	35.4
2 Semesters	45.3	54.6	52.2	50.7
3 Semesters	53.2	59.4	57.6	57.4
4 Semesters	60.1	63.8	63.1	63.7
	Means for Public Secondary Schools			
1 Semester	26.3	31.2	32.0	27.5
2 Semesters	41.8	47.2	47.5	45.0
3 Semesters	50.3	54.2	53.4	53.0
4 Semesters	57.6	60.1	58.8	59.8

year. As was to be expected, our pupils make their poorest
showing as compared with the norms in the section on
grammar and their best in that on vocabulary. Though, as
was indicated earlier, they had been given some exposure
to formal grammar in anticipation of tests of this sort, this
experience had been brief. We were, consequently, pleased
that the averages stood up as well in this section as they did.
In fact, since the test is not appropriate to the kind of training our students had had, we were pleased with all the
scores, though they appear unimpressive.

As usual, the wide range of achievement within the group
is worth noting. Some students are achieving at almost the
level of four semesters of high-school work, even on this
inappropriate test; others in the group fall far short of the
equivalent of even one semester. In this connection one
point in regard to the effects of sectioning are worth comment. As has been indicated in chapters 4 and 5, when sectioning was instituted in the third year of the program, the
principle was applied much less rigorously to this group

of fourth-grade starters than it was to the third-grade starters. Thus, the regular sections of the fourth-grade group
always contained many weaker students than did the regular section of the third-grade starters. But the presence of
these less able students does not seem, at least in any obvious way, to have impeded the progress of the better students in this group. As we have just seen, they performed
surprisingly well.

Because of the time devoted to other testing during the
fourth year of the program, time was not stolen from instruction in order to administer the Listening Test. Hence,
for this group we have no terminal measure on a standardized test of this group's achievement in aural comprehension. On various grounds, we believe it was as good or
better than that reported earlier in this chapter for the
third-grade starters. Informal measures point in that direction. And, in the following year, when the remnants of this
group were measured in high school, 73 per cent of them
fell in the upper quarter of the percentile norms for two
years' work in private secondary schools.

Their ratings on accuracy of pronunciation were similar
to those of the third-grade group: Excellent 41 per cent,
Good 54 per cent, Fair 5 per cent, and Poor 0 per cent.
Thus, nearly all of them acquired a "good" or "excellent"
pronunciation as a result of their FLES experience, one of
the major purposes of the program.

Looking at the results for both groups, we are fairly well
pleased. With new materials and new staff and with almost
no access to audio-visual aids for this group, the results
might well have been disappointing. As it was, the fluency
and accuracy of the children's speech as compared with
that of high-school and college beginners has always been
impressive. Their ability to understand the spoken language too has been more than satisfactory. The results on
such measures as the Co-operative Test have been somewhat disappointing. Though we were well aware that such
measures were unfair to our program, we had originally

hoped that we would enable our students to accomplish more than we did in regard to these traditional objectives. We were overly ambitious in regard to, among other things, the way in which the birds of reading and grammar can be killed with a single FLES stone. Lack of time is perhaps the fundamental factor here. While the language skills are interrelated and do re-enforce each other, the fact remains that at the early stages when a student is practicing one skill he is not actually practicing the others. But though the students did not do as well as we had sanguinely hoped, their achievement, in our opinion, is satisfactory.

With revised materials, more experienced staff, and access to a modern language laboratory which is now available, probably the level of achievement will rise somewhat in future years. But we doubt whether these or other improvements will raise the level markedly. Performance will stay about as it is. And that is good enough.

8 articulation with the high school

From the outset we had firmly believed that "continuity" must be a major principle of FLES instruction. This term means something slightly different at different points on the educational ladder, but we were convinced that both senses of the term were of primary importance.

Within the elementary years continuity means primarily the uninterrupted, cumulative development of skills and knowledge in relation to some one language and culture. The preceding chapters have shown how we sought to produce this development within the FLES program.

But continuity also means a smooth transition from FLES

to the work of high school and college. If the skills developed in the FLES program are ignored or neglected in the secondary school, waste is certain. The time and effort put into FLES are wasted insofar as unused knowledge and unpracticed skills deteriorate rapidly. At the same time the secondary-school program itself is less efficient and extensive than it could be if it built upon the foundation already laid by FLES. Only a continuous program covering four or five elementary grades and two or more years of high school seems likely to bring the student to that degree of mastery where he can speak, understand, read, and write the language with some ease and accuracy. Only this level of linguistic command will enable the student who wishes to continue his study of French into college to devote himself there to the kind of language work suited to his level of interest and maturity — literature and composition — or enable the pupil who terminates his study somewhere in the high-school period to use the language easily for cultural or practical purposes.

Our experience with this latter sort of continuity is limited to the immediate transition to high school. Even here our experience is relatively slight since it is limited to two classes. Our students who began French in the fourth grade entered high school in 1959 after four years of FLES; those who began in the third grade entered high school in 1960 after five years of FLES.

Though we had foreseen the general problem of articulation from the beginning, we had underestimated its complexity. We had, of course, anticipated that we should have to make some kind of appropriate provision for our FLES products at the high-school level. We had also seen that we would need some preparation within our FLES program for later work in high school as is indicated by our provision of some work in formal grammar. But we had rather vaguely envisaged our FLES graduates as a fairly uniform group of students, who, as a result of their four or five years of experience, would be fairly fluent and accurate in speaking, would have considerable ability at aural comprehension, and some skill in reading. We assumed that primarily we would need one new high-school course which would further exploit the gains already made in the audio-lingual areas, would give further skill in reading, and would introduce formal grammar and writing. We also hoped that this course would constitute sufficient special provision to permit later amalgamation of FLES students with regular high school classes at some level — with relief from all the problems of special sectioning and scheduling for FLES students.

The problem has been more complicated than expected. Not that we were ignorant of any of the factors which have produced these complications. They have just been more influential than we had originally thought was likely.

They can be briefly recapitulated here in terms of their influence on the problem of articulation.

Differences in amount of achievement. — Though we had naturally expected considerable spread in achievement growing out of individual differences in capacity and application, we had not been prepared for the enormous range which developed after four or five years of instruction. Even the grossest classification produced at least three groups: students reaping maximum benefit and performing extremely well, those doing reasonably well, and those gaining little or nothing from FLES. Thus, instead of having to provide for one group, we found ourselves with, at the very least, three.

Differences in kind of achievement. — There is considerable variation among students not merely in the amount of achievement but in the kind or area of achievement. For example, some respond well to aural-oral work; others do not, but find reading or grammar more congenial. Some react favorably to concrete tasks (projects, plays, home assignments); others detest them. Thus any one of the three general levels of achievement shows in the case of any particular pupil considerable variation in respect to the various specific skills and the rest.

Differences in exposure to the language. — Transfer students (at least in our situation) cause considerable difficulty for a program extending over so long a span. If the students in a program are actually learning anything, it should be difficult for a newcomer to enter after a year or two. But in ways mentioned earlier, it was not too difficult to take care of transfer students who entered after only the first year or two. Those entering in the last year or two of the program, however, presented a more difficult problem. The better ones of them might fairly soon become better than the worst of our regular students but they could not easily catch up with those of average achievement.

In short, we were confronted by a considerably more heterogeneous group (or a larger number of fairly distinct groups) than we had originally anticipated.

In addition, certain other considerations in regard to "continuity" were involved. On the one hand, we had at the outset asked students and parents to commit themselves, certainly to the full span of the FLES program, and preferably to considerable continuation of it in high school. We were naturally interested to see the extent to which the FLES program would interest students in further French in high school. On the other hand, as the preceding pages make clear, it seemed quite evident that some students should not continue to take French to no purpose. Faced with a two-year language requirement in the high school, these students would do better either to start another language by a somewhat different method, (whether immediately or after the wait of a year or two) or to ask for some mitigation of the language requirement. We were, therefore, equally interested to see whether the recommendation to discontinue French would be followed. Since certain status considerations had become connected with the foreign-language work, there was some possibility that students, who on all other grounds would have done well to drop French, might be inclined to continue.

Our first group to enter high school consisted of those students who were already in the fourth grade at the start of our program. Though these students are not typical of our program in that they had only four rather than five years of FLES, they are illustrative of the problems and the possible solutions. These students were divided into four categories.

Category I. These were the students who had demonstrated superior achievement and were to be encouraged to continue French during their Freshman year in order to take full advantage of the possibility of an additional four years of work in high school. Out of a total of twenty-two students in this category, all except one followed our recommendation and took French in the special section provided for them. All are also continuing French in their Sophomore year (1960–61). The one student who did not continue with French has re-enrolled in a regular beginning French course in 1960–61.

Category II. These were students whose performance had been only adequate or were transfer students who started French after the fourth grade. Of the twenty-six students for whom continuing French in their Freshman year was suggested, twenty-two chose to stay with French as freshmen in a special section provided for them and are continuing it as sophomores. Two students changed to Latin and are now (1960–61) in their second year of it. Two students dropped foreign language in 1959–60, but one of them has resumed French in 1960–61.

Category III. These students were not encouraged to continue foreign language study because of their mediocre achievement. Of these fifteen students, two disregarded our recommendation and continued with French in the section for students in Category II, two shifted to Latin, and the rest dropped language for the year 1959–60. For the year 1960–61, five of the dropouts are back in French,

133

three switched to German, and three are still taking no foreign language.

Category IV. This group was composed of students who had, over the FLES period, indicated lack of aptitude or interest in languages or who, having recently transferred into our school, had had relatively little contact. This group was urged to defer foreign language instruction until the Sophomore year or to try a different language. Of these nineteen students, two disregarded our recommendation and continued French in 1959–60 in a regular beginning class. The other seventeen temporarily dropped foreign language, but we find them registered as sophomores in regular beginning classes as follows: French (ten), German (one), Latin (one), no foreign language (five).

In looking at this behavior on the part of a class which had one year less than our full FLES program, we find considerable ground for satisfaction. The better students, some forty-five of them, were interested in going on with their French. By this time they are adding a second year of high-school work to their four FLES years and by virtue of their early start should be well on the way to an adequate command of the language. It is this sort of result which we see as the major merit of FLES.

But we think it important also to note the response of those with whom we were less successful, even those with whom we essentially failed. As can readily be seen from the preceding figures, even an unsuccessful experience in FLES has not led to the attitude, "I'm through with French." This reaction seemed to us a likely possibility, and one which would be a legitimate ground for concern. Yet when the majority of these students resume the study of a foreign language, they again take French. In informal conversations they state their feelings in such expressions as, "We're bound to cash in on the little we got in grade school" or "This time we're really going to get it." Thus their earlier experience has not produced a negative attitude toward French and seems even to have had some positive consequences in teaching them something about the nature and value of intellectual effort.

Pupils beginning our program in the third grade and taking the full five years of FLES are our other group to make the transition into high school. Though they are more representative of our product, we can, of course, follow them only into the current year as freshmen.

All the students in Group A (who completed the program as planned and on schedule) are continuing French if they remained in the school for the present year. They are grouped in a special section designed to build on the skills they have already acquired and to remedy defects or gaps in their previous training.

There are also two other special sections for former FLES students. Each of them has about ten pupils who began in the third grade. But these are the students from Group B, which went at the slightly slower pace. These sections are brought up to regular size (20–25) by the addition of transfer students who entered the program at various early stages and who made sufficient progress to work along with these less able students from the original group. Finally, three members of the original group and the remaining transfer students (who either entered the program very late or for some other reason achieved very little proficiency) are continuing their French by going back to a regular beginners' class in the high school.

Thus each year our FLES program has committed our high-school program to three special sections to handle our FLES students. This prodecure obviously complicates our scheduling and programming. It is not, however, as expensive as might appear at first glance. Since most of the sections can run at full size and since instruction in language would be provided for them in any case, offering appropriate classes rather than just any classes involves additional cost only in those few instances where sections are small. But the scheduling problem is admittedly vexing. We see, however, no alternative to this procedure if we are to make a linguistically oriented FLES program maximally effective. Our problem is, of course, simplified by the fact that both elementary and secondary programs are "under the same management." The high-school classes have to deal with the products of only one FLES program, the nature of which is known. In more confused situations, the problem is inevitably greater and the solutions less satisfactory.

In sum, granting that our situation is particularly fortunate in some respects, we are generally well pleased with the continuity by which our program has been marked. Four or five years of FLES followed by two years of work in high school (we hope members of our "A Groups" will continue for four years) should give our pupils a command of the language for which neither we nor they need apologize.

notes to chapter 8

P. 130. *Transition from FLES.* — The desirability of continuity between elementary-school and high-school language instruction is universally acknowledged. Since few programs have operated long enough in situations where continuity could be observed and measured, most discussions of the problem raise questions or stress possibilities rather than report experience. The following articles are useful: Emile B. De Sauzé, "Continuity and Articulation in the Study of Foreign Languages between Elementary and Senior High School," *French Review,* XXVIII (May, 1955), 536–37; Marian Dryer, "Grade School French Students Reach High School," *French Review*, XXIX (December, 1955), 157–61; Manuel H. Guerra, "New FLES Adventures and the Villain of Articulation," *Modern Language Journal*, XLII (November, 1958), 320–24.

One obvious possible solution, special high-school courses for students with FLES experience, is vastly complicated by the wide range of objectives and levels of achievement which mark various FLES programs. As a result, a high school drawing students from several different programs, can hardly know in advance what sort of previous experience to anticipate on the part of its entrants. In these situations little more can be done than to place FLES students in regular classes and allow them to distinguish themselves by their superior accent, fluency, and motivation, and their more rapid progress.

9   problems and conclusions

Working with all aspects of a FLES program for five years has been a stimulating and rewarding experience. By and large, we are well pleased with the results. As the preceding pages and some of our earlier reports made evident, we set ourselves very ambitious goals — probably overambitious ones. In part we did so because we accepted too trustingly exaggerated claims often made for the linguistic ability of the child. In part we did so because we felt it desirable that our experiment should aim high. Falling short of even impossible goals seemed likely to produce a better level of achievement than merely hoping that by some happy accident an unexpected increment would crown a more diffident effort. We believed that both the students and we were more likely to respond to a distinct challenge.

We have tried to make clear the points at which our hopes were disappointed. Nonetheless, with all due allowance for inexact data, inappropriate measuring devices, unsolved problems, and some students who achieved little or nothing, we believe the results give us objective grounds for satisfaction.

For many of our students, French has been a pleasant and highly profitable experience. They have entered high school at the second-year level or beyond. We believe they achieved a better pronunciation and a greater fluency than they would otherwise have gained, and they now have four additional years in high school in which to consolidate this good beginning to whatever degree they choose. Because our tests were not always suited to FLES students, we believe that our students were actually better than the measures reveal. But we are willing to rest on the objective results. The fact that the FLES program in the school has been expanded to include German (with Russian and Spanish currently being considered) constitutes rather clear evidence that the faculty and administration find that the initial FLES venture in French had merit.

Without attempting to recapitulate the preceding chapters in a few paragraphs here, the following points are those on which our opinion is fairly firm as a result of our own experience and the information we have about other programs.

A successful FLES program demands three major prerequisites. (1.) The administration must be prepared to furnish both financial and moral support. (2.) A staff competent to teach the language and to work with elementary-school pupils must be assembled and maintained. This staff must include at least one member willing and able to assume primary responsibility and to offer leadership. (3.) Only wholehearted co-operation from the entire school faculty will make possible meaningful integration of FLES materials with other subjects and provide the climate of good will necessary if the trying problems of scheduling and the rest are to be adequately solved.

Other factors like student interest and parental support are also important, but these elements tend to be products or consequences of the preceding three. As we indicated earlier, the development of audio-visual aids may make it possible to use a less competent staff. But at present these ventures appear what the stock market calls "speculative": they may pay off or they may, unless used with discretion, produce dubious results.

Operational problems like staffing and scheduling are enormous, but they can be solved provided that the general faculty and the administration as well as the foreign language group are sincerely interested in the success of the program and will devote the time and energy to evolving satisfactory solutions. A program sufficiently flexible to be good will inevitably generate a host of such problems. Since they are impossible to avoid, effort is best directed toward producing a context in which they can be solved.

FLES is justified by both the qualitative and quantitative benefits it confers. By "qualitative" we mean that the pupil in the early elementary grades has a chance to acquire the oral skills to a degree probably not attainable if he starts later. If being able to speak the foreign language with maximum fluency and accuracy of pronunciation are proper objectives for foreign language study, FLES makes a contribution which may be unique.

By "quantitative" we mean that FLES provides a span of additional years during which the pupil can work with the language. As we have indicated, we had hoped that on the basis of actual hours of contact with the language, this increment from an early start would be larger in regard to some of the skills than it in fact proved to be. In general, however, our better students have had the equivalent of two high-school years of French at the grade-school level.

140

It thus comes at a stage where they are particularly able to profit from exposure to the foreign language; conversely, those who do not wish longer experience with French can put the later time, thus freed, to some other use.

When the audio-lingual skills are a major objective, students in the third and fourth grade do better than those beginning later. Our opinion on this point rests on considerable observation and impression in addition to such limited evidence as we were able to present in chapter 6. When the foreign language is studied as a school subject in a program like ours, the fourth graders do as well or better than the third graders in the oral skills. Since we are not speaking here of the child who acquires the foreign language by living in the milieu where it is spoken, we suspect that the better progress of the fourth grader is due to greater maturity, better adjustment to school routines, or similar characteristics which make the fourth graders somewhat better able to profit from formal classroom work. Though we have no personal experience, we are not impressed by the possibilities (for a program of our sort) of a still earlier beginning. For programs otherwise oriented the judgment might be different, but for serious progress toward language mastery in the formal situation, we doubt whether the gains would justify the additional time, effort, and money expended.

We are convinced that not all third or fourth graders can profit from a course aimed primarily at mastering the language skills and that this fact is sufficiently evident by the end of the first FLES year. We are concerned over the fate of those children who are obviously having difficulty at this point yet who are apparently doomed to four or five years of failure and frustrations. Two alternatives are possible. Subsequent language work should be provided for them in a course which stresses other possible FLES objectives. In this case all concerned (general faculty, administration, pupils, parents, and language staff) should be clear what these objectives are and what their place in the total school program is. The second alternative suggests that the time and effort of these pupils should be employed in something other than language work.

We are equally convinced that for the majority of students at this stage in the elementary school, FLES is a true opportunity. Though we admit that we may be prejudiced, we feel that the opportunity to study a foreign language has claims analogous to those advanced by science, mathematics, and other studies to which pupils are introduced in the elementary school. Though not all students will later make great use of these subjects, all should have the opportunity to discover their capacities. And for those who are capable in these areas, not offering an early introduction is an unfair and possibly irremediable neglect. Moreover, insofar as it can be shown that children of this age have a special capacity for the audio-lingual skills and can in fact profit from foreign-language work at this age, language study has some claims to priority at this point. The question may be at least raised whether some other subjects could not be studied as well, or even more effectively, when the pupils are older.

In sum, then, we believe that FLES programs make real contributions which can be demonstrated to some degree — a degree, incidentally, not much inferior, if at all, to that open to similar demonstration by all elementary-school subjects.

But to say that FLES is good is not to deny that it can and should be made better. Since we do not belong to that wing of the profession which apparently feels that the acknowledgment of problems or doubts is a form of treason, we should like to mention specifically the following problems. These are major difficulties which will not be solved easily. But improved solutions must be found for them if FLES programs are to succeed in the long run and in a variety of situations.

We need a more adequate battery of tests which will accurately measure the achievement of FLES students and

142

make possible their accurate placement in high school as well as a precise comparison with other FLES and high-school groups. Because of the nature of our own program, we have emphasized in the preceding pages the need for better tests of the audio-lingual skills as developed by FLES. But the need is no less pressing in other areas, perhaps even more so. For example, if FLES is primarily to overcome a monolingual, monocultural attitude, it is important that there be measuring devices and experimental evidence which will make possible some demonstration that such results are obtained and obtained to a greater degree or with greater efficiency than is possible otherwise.

The present lack of such instruments is not due merely to inadvertence on the part of the profession. Rather grave difficulties stand in the way of even a fairly satisfactory program. For example, the tests of oral skills must be individual. For individual tests to attain objective reliability and practical feasibility in the elementary-school situation involves almost insurmountable complications. Tests to measure change in attitudes or cultural awareness offer different but no less difficult problems. Moreover, it is a familiar phenomenon that everyone wants tests which measure everything his students know and ask absolutely nothing which has not fallen within the local course of study. In view of the diversity of courses familiar on the American educational scene, such precision is impossible. But it is to be hoped that some "injustice" rather than a rigidly uniform program or complete lack of evidence concerning what is, in fact, being accomplished will be preferred. Until objective measures for major FLES objectives of all sorts are available and used, statements about FLES, pro or con, must possess very limited validity.

We need a much greater mass of carefully prepared materials of all sorts to give the FLES student additional contact with the language and to lead from one skill to another.

This need begins with films and tapes to extend the student's audio-lingual experience. Then, if reading is ever to be introduced, the need arises for an assortment of reading materials which are related to the audio-lingual materials in which the FLES student is versed and which lie within his competence. Finally if the FLES student is to do more than merely mimic the basic patterns he has learned and employ a few simple variants on them which may not get him into trouble, he needs something more appropriate than the traditional high-school grammars to lead him into a knowledge of the structure of the language.

The materials just mentioned are all needed for mastery of the language skills. We speak with more diffidence concerning the materials needed for other FLES objectives since these areas have been only ancillary to our major work. But as interested bystanders, we are skeptical whether great progress will be made toward those other ends as major objectives without a greater bulk of more carefully prepared materials than those which have come to our attention thus far.

In all respects we need much better facilities to deal with the individual student. (1.) We need much better ways of determining when the student is ready for FLES and what kind of FLES program he is ready for. (2.) Once he is in a program, we need much greater flexibility to provide for his particular capabilities and interests. Though the needed materials just mentioned constitute a large part of this need, greater flexibility of programming and approach (which are still more difficult to provide than the materials which are an integral part of them) will be demanded. To be able to discover how a particular pupil can best acquire FLES objectives, to have the wherewithal to use this approach and to have the flexibility to employ it, — to have all these will make FLES more effective than it has been.

We need much more research at all levels, both the laboratory exploration of the fundamentals of language learning and the classroom examination of various procedures and methods. Better measuring devices are, of course, the

144

sine qua non here. Without more demonstrated theory and more carefully examined practice, FLES programs will continue to explore blind alleys and waste students' time by trial and error.

In addition to these rather "material" needs, workers in FLES have another set of needs, less tangible but no less vital.

We need to realize that FLES is due for many more years of growing pains. Though excellence is the goal, achievement short of it is likely. But such results should be a basis for renewed constructive effort rather than grounds for dismay, defeatism, or "scapegoating."

We need to recognize that FLES is still in its embryonic state and will probably develop into a variety of different forms. Consequently, all categorical statements from "authorities" are at best guide lines and hypotheses, and experiments and deviations from such dogmas are not unpardonable heresies. To adapt such directives to specific situations and to his own capacities and predilections is the prerogative (and even the responsibility) of the teacher, which he should exercise with intelligence and confidence.

We need to acknowledge that FLES cannot be all things to all people, that it need not be the sole area of the elementary curriculum where success is guaranteed and where individual differences in aptitude and ability are assumed to present no problems. "Non-achievers" in FLES should be a cause of concern but not of consternation, and administrators, scrutinizing FLES especially because it is something of a novelty, must remember that individual differences in achievement — with some at the low end of the distribution — will appear when anything is taught.

We need to perceive FLES as a justifiable part of the elementary curriculum on the basis of the kind of learning experience it provides, calling for attentiveness, perseverance and a capacity to await a deferred reward — attitudes which the teacher can strive to develop but which are not always a heritage of the "gifted," nor are they promoted by the general orientation of every school or school system.

We need to be more explicit about what we can achieve in a given situation so that results can be measured in terms of fairly specific goals rather than on the basis of vague hopes or nebulous inferences.

We need to communicate the fact that many of the important outcomes of FLES are about as intangible as many of these needs. In addition to broadening the child's horizons in regard to language and culture and giving him some command of the language, we are producing students who study language beyond the required years, students who look forward to visiting the people whose language they have mastered, students who are considering making language their life work.

In short, FLES programs, whether now or ever, are guaranteed neither miracles nor flops. Like every other subject in the elementary curriculum, FLES is a continual challenge to all of us to provide the richest possible educational experience for a wide variety of pupils.

index